AF292567

Kayla Jade is a digital creator and writer with a highly engaged, predominantly female audience across TikTok and Instagram. She first built her platform on OnlyFans, later catapulting her reach on TikTok, where her candid takes on dating, sex, identity and the realities of modern womanhood have earned her a fiercely loyal community.

Her rise has been covered by major media outlets including SBS, ABC, *The Guardian* and *Pedestrian*. She has also appeared on leading podcasts such as *It's A Lot with Abbie Chatfield* and *Big Small Talk* with Hannah Ferguson, and hosts her own top-charting show, *Storytime with Kayla Jade*.

As a creator, she has partnered with key brands including Grill'd, Honey Birdette and Vush, with whom she released her own custom-designed sex toy.

Known online as Blue Eyed Kayla Jade, she now reaches more than 3.5 million women across platforms and has built a community defined by humour, honesty and unwavering relatability.

Call Girl Confidential is her debut book.

Names, places and occupations have been changed to protect clients and because: 'If you break this NDA, it will cost you five times what you earn in a year.' – Anon.

Content note: this book contains descriptions of sexual violence and disordered eating.

Call Girl Confidential

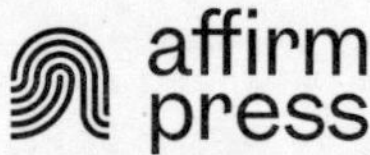

First published in Australia in 2026 by Affirm Press,
a Simon & Schuster (Australia) Pty Limited company
Wurundjeri Woiwurrung Country
Level 3, 162 Collins Street, Melbourne VIC 3000

Affirm Press is located on the unceded land of the Wurundjeri Woiwurrung peoples
of the Kulin Nation. Affirm Press pays respect to their Elders past and present.

New York Amsterdam/Antwerp London Toronto Sydney/Melbourne New Delhi
Visit our website at www.simonandschuster.com.au

AFFIRM PRESS and design are trademarks of Affirm Press Pty Ltd, Inc., used under
licence by Simon & Schuster, LLC.

A catalogue record for this
book is available from the
National Library of Australia

978-1-76182-315-2 (paperback)
9781761822520 (ebook)

Cover design by Luke Causby/Blue Cork
All cover images by Gracie Steindl
Typeset by J&M Typesetting in 12/19 pt Garamond Premier Pro
Printed and bound by CPI Group (UK) Ltd, Croydon CR0 4YY

The authorised representative in the EEA is Simon & Schuster Netherlands BV,
Herculesplein 96, 3584 AA Utrecht, Netherlands. info@simonandschuster.nl

Call Girl Confidential

Blue-Eyed Kayla Jade

affirm press

CONTENTS

Prologue

I force myself to make eye contact. The guy in the loin cloth is crawling on all fours towards me, occasionally growling and swiping the air with his clawed hand. But I can't help it – my gaze keeps dropping to his groin. Are they ... *tiger stripes*? Yeah. So what exactly is he going for here? Tarzan or tiger? Or the lovechild of both?

I'm always getting distracted.

My reaction should be the same either way: '*Mmm.*' A trademark moan that dissolves into a giggle.

While he looks ridiculous in his loin cloth, it's nothing compared to how I feel in his chosen outfit for me. The metallic g-string is designed to stretch up to the shoulders, mankini-style, with the result of giving me a camel-toe wedgie. Is he actually trying to humiliate me?

I shift in my seat. To be more accurate, I am astride a saddle. A black horse saddle, strapped all the way under the mattress to keep it in place. Given the man's weird moods, I imagine the tantrum he would have had, trying to heave the king-size mattress around and wrestle those straps together. With the number of sex toys and costumes he has on call, this isn't his first rodeo. In fact, I will later find out, it is his mission to fuck and film every OnlyFans girl on the Gold Coast. A collector, if you will.

It seems odd to me that the saddle needs be so firmly strapped. Gingerly, I wiggle the dildo I am impaled upon by giving a little bounce of my butt. The black phallus seems sturdily affixed.

'*Rrrraow,*' the man says, reaching the base of the bed. With a demonic grin, he flicks a switch on the floor. I hadn't noticed the cord running south of the saddle. With a violent jerk, the dildo cranks to life. Oh my god, it's a fucking machine. Like, a machine that fucks. I've seen this in videos but nothing could prepare me for the absolute—

'Fuuuuuck!' I scream, over the deafening motor. The dildo pistons so vigorously that diners in the hotel restaurant downstairs must be frowning up at the flickering lights. If only they knew.

The client doesn't miss a beat, grabbing his cock and pumping it furiously as the dildo pummels my insides.

How did I get here? I think, not for the first time. And also: *Think of the money. Think of the money. Think of the money.*

Being Broke

Are you familiar with the particular shade of despair that comes with never being able to make ends meet? It takes the shine off the world around you. My despair turned the Gold Coast's turquoise waters to grey, joggers' whitened teeth into mean snarls, the yachts bobbing outside bayside restaurants into personal insults. My car's back bumper was held on with duct tape after a prang at one of the Gold Coast's endless sets of traffic lights. I would change the tape every two weeks to make it look pristine, but nothing could fix the anxiety I felt about running that car on fumes, only ever putting $20 into the tank when the red warning light was flashing.

Aged nineteen, I'd moved to Australia from small-town New Zealand specifically to make something of myself. And yet here I was, five years later, living pay cheque to pay cheque, working shitty-ass jobs I hated, completely unable to save any money. And I didn't even have expensive tastes yet.

Palmerston North is on New Zealand's North Island, 140 kilometres from the nearest city, Wellington, and a million miles from anything exciting. Growing up there, I felt sheltered. Not in a cosy way, but in the sense that sex was considered taboo and shameful: almost as shameful as having ideas above your station. People who grew up in Palmy rarely went far beyond its borders, and that feeling of being stifled meant the bottle shops and drug dealers did a good trade. There was a cross-generational malaise. Dad's boozing probably gave my teenage antics a good run for their money.

I wouldn't say we were dirt poor, but I come from a lower-middle-class family. Mum worked long hours as a cook at a cafe chain that sold hot breakfasts: waffles, baked goods, that kind of thing. Dad was a plasterer, always chasing jobs. The family home was a pretty ordinary weatherboard in the town centre of Palmerston North, surrounded by the usual small-town staples: bottle shop, every franchise of pizza takeaway, panelbeaters, motels. There were a few white picket fences on our street, because people do like to make an effort, but that's where the aspirations seemed to end. Palmy wasn't a town I wanted to be born and die in. As soon as I was old enough, I wanted to know what else was out there ... and also to let the heat cool down a bit in Palmy. I'd been getting into some trouble – but that's a story for later.

I'd been to the Gold Coast before as a teenager, with my mum and sister, who's seven years older than me. Touching down at the airport, I gawked at the billboard ads for Dracula's, the local dinner theatre experience. Before we'd even left the terminal I was getting the sense that the Gold Coast was an intoxicating blend of naff and glam. The idea of glamour was new to me. My dress sense was pretty grungy and I never saw my mum wear make-up. But, looking around at the tanned, buff people of the GC, I suddenly liked the idea of glowing up: of creating the face, body and wardrobe of someone who was successful. Someone new.

We spent that holiday shopping at the big American-style malls, doing the rounds of theme parks and going to the beach. I couldn't believe that people actually lived here, and were basically living the holiday life 365 days a year. The glitter from that trip would take a while to wear off.

So it seemed like a natural choice for me to move to the Gold Coast a couple of years later, particularly as a friend from home was there. The plan was that I would stay six months, then attempt to figure out what I wanted to do with my life. Mainly, it was a deliberate cutting of the umbilical cord to New Zealand.

The reality? I did all the shit jobs. *All* of them. First, I worked in a call centre in Surfers Paradise, hassling people to become members of a hotel chain, but I'm way too go-with-the-flow to be pushy. If someone doesn't want to do something, I'm like, 'Don't do it, dude.' The managers were constantly monitoring us, and my attitude didn't go down well.

My next job was at a surf shop on the Sunshine Coast, which I thought might be more chill, but it was just more of the same. My boss would push me to make sales by hassling people who'd walked in for a browse. I tried to impress upon him that some people just like to look around, and we'd butt heads about that. My ADHD can make me quite defiant, particularly if someone tries to tell me what to do. I was also having to wing my way through conversations with customers, since I didn't surf. I'd overhear one guy saying something about the swell that morning and then I'd just repeat that nugget to whoever else came in. *Hmmm ... I'm quite good at bluffing,* I realised. My brain packed that fact away for later.

Sick of lurking behind customers, I decided to study to be a personal trainer. I liked the idea of helping people achieve their dreams, even if mine were dead at the side of the road. I hadn't even finished my certification when I managed to talk my way into a job at a gym. *Wow*, I thought. *Okay, so this is what I do now*. And people believed me. It seemed I was very good at being a mirror to other people, showing them what they wanted to see. Like every other job, though, this one bit the dust when I started clashing with the owner about hours and conditions.

One thing was becoming clear: if I was going to succeed in life, I was going to have to be my own boss.

~

To really profit as a sex worker, you have to be willing to morph into whatever fantasy the client desires. You need to be able to read people and to shapeshift on your feet. I had those skills, but they were wasted in the jobs I'd been doing.

Despite what you might be thinking, I'm absolutely not afraid of hard work, not when it's something I'm passionate about. At high school I was an A-grade student, hyperfocused on being perfect. I loved science and maths especially, but I was determined to get my head across every subject. Looking back, I wonder if I was using study to distract myself from the fact that I was developing hardcore anorexia. Both the push for perfect grades and the push for thinness required me to be a hard grafter: someone driven and self-directed. Back then, it was unhealthy; but what if that work ethic could be harnessed in a better way?

Money has always been a major motivation. I got my first job in a supermarket deli at fifteen and was quickly promoted to seafood manager. Woo! Yeah, I know, but it did ignite a fire in me to climb higher. I just didn't know in which field yet. I left school at seventeen so I could work (and earn) full-time. There was never a push from my family for me to go to university, but I did get part way through a Bachelor of Nutrition – my interest in which, perversely, was influenced by my eating disorder.

It was during the pandemic that I started thinking about OnlyFans. The platform had been launched in 2016 but it was during the pandemic that its profile rocketed, thanks to women around the world being in lockdown: broke and bored. Creators were posting videos and nudes, and doing livestreams to a bunch of thirsty subscribers, who would happily pay for different tiers of access. There was no need to work for a boss, or even leave the house. I started following several popular female creators on OnlyFans, studying them like I was back at school pursuing perfect grades. How did they get followers? What made them successful and other creators not so?

I should make clear at this point that I love sex. I'm a very freaky girl. I've experimented widely with different kinks, and with men and women. Unlike at home in Palmy, sex was out in the open in Australia – especially on the Gold Coast. Lots of Australian porn stars were based on the GC, and I noticed that many OnlyFans girls were, too. Maybe it's down to the warm climate and laidback culture: locals are used to wearing bikinis or going shirtless, and the aesthetic here is distinctly sexy, like Miami or Rio. Even the place names resemble those kinds of places: Surfers Paradise, Mermaid Waters, Paradise Point, Palm Beach. It's like a playground for Barbies and Kens. At least it is if you have money.

At this point, in 2021, OnlyFans was worth US$1billion and had around 120 million users. How could I possibly make my mark? I made good use of my ADHD hyperfocus and made it my mission to game the system, determining to launch in January 2022. New year, new me, right? Isn't that what the women's mags always say?

Baby Daddy

I can't fully get to my sexcapades without bringing in the baby daddy and his role in all this. People around the world, in chats and in comments, have searched for evidence of this man like true-crime sleuths, so I'll introduce him now so that they can stop tripping.

I matched with Jackson on Tinder about three weeks after I moved to Australia and, unlike everything else that was going on in my life, it was the easiest thing in the world. When you know, you know.

I'd found a share house in Mermaid Beach, but already I was dying to get out of there. One flatmate was a massive dude who only ever hit pause on gaming in his bedroom to accept a fast food Uber Eats delivery or sell drugs to a late-night visitor. And then there was a couple in their thirties who bored me to tears with their total commitment to fitness and steroids. It was quite the Gold Coast baptism, if you believe the stereotypes.

One night, I was lying on my bed swiping out of sheer boredom, when I matched with Jackson. Dark hair, dark eyes, good-looking, a few tattoos. A little bit alternative, which I like, but with good-dude vibes, which would be a novel experience for me. This guy was studying a Bachelor of Social Welfare. That didn't scream skeezy psychopath to me. Although … it's always the quiet ones.

Our first date was a Saturday night. Jackson picked me up in his grandmother's old Mercedes. It was pale blue, on its last legs, and the back seat was littered with his books and uni papers. I settled into the sagging front passenger seat and picked at a rip in the sheepskin cover as I checked him out. Thankfully, he was as cute in real life as he was in his pictures. I loved his smile and he had kind eyes. We stopped off at a bottle shop to get some drinks and while we were at the counter I spotted some chewing gum. I decided to get some in case we'd be kissing later. It was an obvious move, reaching for the gum, but I didn't mind planting that kind of thought. Later, much later, after we had indeed pashed, Jackson told me that watching me choose the gum told me everything he needed to know. 'You just grabbed the one from the bottom of the pile without thinking,' he said, 'so that the whole stack was messed up.'

I think he was trying to say that I was excitingly impulsive, but the jury's out.

After the store, we drove to his apartment in Coolangatta to hang out. We'd fully intended to hit a bar later, but instead we wound up talking about music all night, taking turns to play each other YouTube clips on our phones, everything from death metal to rap battles, just bouncing off each other. It was the most eclectic shit, because we have such weird tastes. Childish Gambino, Marilyn Manson … He educated me on Australian hip-hop, which didn't take that long. At some point he strummed his guitar as he talked and I didn't hate it. I used to play guitar too. My guitar teacher also had eclectic tastes, so I decided not to regale Jackson with a rendition of Wet Wet Wet's 'Love Is All Around' – not when we were on such a high.

We became instant soul mates that night and fucked and talked until we couldn't stay awake anymore. Despite being born and bred on the Gold Coast, Jackson is the complete opposite of everything it stands for. A lot of what you encounter here has that veneer of phoniness, but he's modest and humble. His dad's Italian-American and his mum had a rural Queensland upbringing, so he never smoothly fitted in. He grew up riding motorbikes and four-wheelers, camping and wakeboarding, but he's also a huge reader and deep thinker.

We hung out all Sunday and then I stayed that night, too, because I couldn't face going back to the share house. 'I'm just gonna stay here now,' I told him, only half-joking. But eventually I couldn't put off going to work any longer, so he dropped me off at the call centre halfway into my Monday shift. For a day or two we didn't see each other, and then I found myself hunched over my phone at my desk, texting the words that would take it to another level: 'I think I'm getting withdrawals.'

So, once again, Jackson picked me up in the Nanna-Merc and I spent another night at his. When it came time to drive me to work the next morning, the car wouldn't start, which we decided was a sign. Jackson told me I was quitting that job, to which I readily agreed. We confessed that we already loved each other. And suddenly my stay in Australia was no longer just a visit.

Okay, now buckle up, because we're about to go V8 on this romance. Me and Baby Daddy moved *fast*. Ariana Grande and Pete Davidson? Halve that.

Jackson was studying from home most days, and we were soon

inseparable. I'd bring him snacks and coax him into bed between lectures. I didn't think I could ever get pregnant. When I was a teenager I'd taken way too many risks but I always got away with it, so I'd made the assumption that I was infertile. But four months into our relationship, my period was late. We bought a pregnancy test from the chemist one evening and decided to do it in the morning, when the results are supposed to be more accurate.

At 4am, I was lying awake. This counted as morning, I decided, so I snuck into the bathroom and weed on the stick. Two pink lines. Pregnant. I ran into our bedroom and woke Jackson. He squinted at the test.

'Oh, okay. Not pregnant,' he said. I opened my eyes even wider and kept holding it in front of him until the penny dropped. He just about screamed – in a good way. We were so excited that as soon as the shops opened we went to the nearest Toys R Us and bought a trolley-load of stuffed animals and toys. Driving back to Jackson's, I attempted to wind down the passenger window and the glass shattered into my lap. The gods were telling us we were broke, but we knew we could make it work, one way or another. We were absolutely infatuated with each other, so obviously we were going to raise the most awesome children.

Seven months into our relationship I was totally blindsided by Jackson's marriage proposal. We'd been living separately for a few months, and not by choice. I was having hellish morning sickness and wanted to be with my mum in New Zealand, but Jackson was doing vocational placements for uni and had to stay on the Goldie. It was hard for us, being so in love. He'd touched down in Wellington, where he'd booked a hotel suite for our romantic reunion, and he'd got all the staff and my family in on the secret; he even rang my mum to ask her permission for my hand.

The first thing I noticed when we opened the hotel door was the smell of scented candles. They were everywhere. On the bed, he'd written in rose petals: *Will you marry me?* Fuck yeah, I would. That was 2015 and it would be another four years – and two children – before we'd actually get the funds to tie the knot. Life, eh?

When we had our first kid I immediately knew I was cut out to be a mum. We named him Benji … although, obviously I've changed our kids' names for this book, so we didn't really. As I was carrying Benji from the hospital to the car, I was so freaked out that the people smoking outside would pollute his perfect little lungs. I wanted to do everything I could to protect this little guy.

By now, Jackson had moved to New Zealand to be with me, but he was only getting offered jobs for about NZ$13 an hour. We were both stressed. So we moved back to Australia and, two years later, we had our daughter, Katie. With our family complete, we decided we couldn't bear to wait any longer to get married.

Jackson wanted a low-key wedding, but nothing about me is low-key, so he just had to accept that. I told him he was doing a speech, but that was the least of his problems, because I also wanted us to wow everyone with a choreographed dance. He chose 'Oh! Darling' by the Beatles and we spent months having formal lessons on Monday nights, with friends minding the kids, so that we could waltz our way through it on the big day. Jackson couldn't listen to 'Oh! Darling' for a few years after that.

My wedding dress was lace with a corset and a traditional line. I'd found it on a website where you can buy second-hand dresses. This one was in mint condition and was selling for $2500 when it was worth more like ten grand. Since we had no money, that was a huge deal.

The wedding itself was on an island just off the Gold Coast, looking out onto the water. My bridal party arrived by chugga-chugga boat, and Jackson and his posse arrived by speedboat.

After the ceremony we cleared the dancefloor and started busting our moves to 'Oh! Darling'. I'd changed into a sheer and sparkly baby-pink dress with lots of layers, and when Jackson dipped me I accidentally flashed everybody – like, every male relative in the room, with about fifteen people capturing the moment on video. It foreshadowed things to come.

We didn't really get to enjoy the wedding night because, just as we were starting to loosen up after the dance, we went to put the kids to bed and wound up crashing with them. Having ghosted our own wedding, we woke up the next morning in a bed drenched with cold pee. As is our style, we just looked at each other and laughed.

After we married we continued to struggle financially: every day a slog, every rent day, tears. Because we were so young, it got to a point where our relationship collapsed. Still, we made a pact that we would keep things steady for the kids. Neither of us could ever bear to go fifty-fifty, so it was easier for us to live together and both see the kids full-time.

Jackson was super supportive of me doing OnlyFans and helped me set it up. From his teens onwards he's been an anti-establishment, nonconformist kind of guy, and he sees no shame in a strong woman owning her sexuality. Plus, he knows that once I've set my mind on something, I'm gonna do it. He just asked that I would always tell him where I was going and what time I'd be home. If I ever went over time, he'd check in on me. When I got back, I'd tell him everything that happened.

We're like yin and yang. I'm an extrovert and Jackson's an introvert.

When we first met, he'd barely left the house for two weeks. He could quite happily live in a wood cabin by himself, whereas I need to be around people to recharge my battery. But as I get older I've become more insular and I get way more in my head than him, so I can draw from his calmness. I guess I'm an anxious extrovert. I need someone to bounce the highs and lows of my day off.

Eventually Jackson started stepping back from his own work to become more of a stay-at-home dad and study for his master's, which suited our new arrangement perfectly. If I had a late-night booking, he'd get up with the kids in the morning, making the school lunches. I still got up at the same time to see them off, but he'd done all the leg-work. I ended up getting a lot of overseas bookings and doing interstate travel, so it made sense that he was holding the fort. And, to be frank, his pay cheque doesn't make a dent compared to mine. People find our set-up hard to get their heads around, but we're both so chill, and such good friends, it just works. It's still hard for me to comprehend that I wound up having children with someone so 'together'.

When you know, you know.

Gaming the System

The cool thing about OnlyFans is that girls who have absolutely zero experience in the sex industry – who haven't 'paid their dues', if you like – can jump straight in. My only previous brush with sex work came when I was eighteen and was working at a fancy degustation restaurant in Auckland. I'd been given a job front of house, greeting people and sitting them down. I detested it. The managers were painful: so particular and unforgiving of the slightest mistake. I couldn't possibly care about working in that place to the extent that they wanted me to.

As I didn't drive, I'd have a long walk home after a shift. The walk took me past a brothel and a strip club, and each time I tried to peer in the windows, but they were blacked out. In my mind, the brothel was like a saloon bar where sexy ladies hung out in corsets and poured you drinks. I persuaded my boyfriend that we should go in. After my eyes adjusted to the gloom I saw that the reception room had one other punter – an old man – with three girls in cheap-looking, brightly coloured lingerie draped all over him. Evidently he hadn't yet chosen his lucky lady. There was nowhere for us to sit and hang out – no martinis being whisked our way on a plate. All three women turned and stared at us like we really had walked into a Wild West saloon. Tumbleweeds.

'Can I help you?' one of the women asked as she glared at my boyfriend, studiously ignoring me. I guess they didn't like sex tourists, there for the shits and giggles. I can appreciate that now. Awkwardly, we mumbled our apologies and left, exploding into laughter the moment the sunlight hit our faces.

A few days later, after another shitful day at work, I was walking past the strip club and decided I'd try my chances there instead. I was on my own this time, so the manager took me more seriously. This woman was stylishly dressed, with tasteful make-up and her hair upswept. She was nice enough, but brisk: she gave the impression that you wouldn't want to test her patience. In the privacy of her office she got me to stand up and turn around. I was very skinny at the time, but there must have been an appetite for that, because without even asking my age she gave me a job.

'Don't worry if you don't have anything to wear,' she said kindly. 'We can find something for you. Just bring heels. And for god's sake, get a tan – you're pale as an Englishman's ass.'

The next day I showed, still sticky with cheap chemist fake tan, with the distinctive scent of chemicals trailing me. Thankfully, they weren't about to put me straight on the pole, so I was instructed to deliver drinks from the bar to the various tables. Most men were cheap, sitting on a middy of beer. Maybe they had to get back to work soon. Plenty of them found time to ogle me as I walked around self-consciously in lingerie with stockings and heels. Being in the throes of my eating disorder and body dysmorphia, this wasn't helping the complex I had about my shape.

I tried to tune the noise out by focusing on the generic R&B, but by the end of my shift I'd decided this joint wasn't for me. Even so, it had lit some kind of spark. The girls at this club felt way more relatable than the tightly buttoned people working in fine dining.

This all goes a little way to explain why I saw no shame in being an OnlyFans creator and instead saw its huge potential for tapping my creativity. That Christmas in lockdown, in 2021, I threw myself into studying the system. This was before there were YouTube tutorials about what to do, so I had to learn everything by trial and error: how to make a profile; how to take good photos and how to light them; what to wear; how to pose; when to post; how to spruik myself on other sites such as Reddit; and how much I could post to TikTok without getting banned. Historically, I'd always struggled with finishing a task – though I was excellent at starting them – but this was different. I became obsessed. For the first time, I was truly passionate about a job.

I knew that people viewed women on OnlyFans as sex workers, even if those women called themselves content creators or media managers. That was okay by me. To succeed on this platform would mean making videos of myself masturbating and eventually having sex with other creators – which we call 'collabs'. In my eyes that was definitely sex work, it just wasn't 'full service' – direct physical contact – because I wasn't meeting any of the subscribers in real life.

The only thing holding me back was fear of judgement, but after a lot of thought I decided to harness that ADHD defiance and use my real first name and never hide my face. Sex was nothing to be ashamed of, and if other people wanted to shame me, that was on them. Some friends did freak out about the idea of me putting videos out there. 'How are you going to feel in ten years' time?' they'd say. But times have changed.

People forget that Paris Hilton and Kim Kardashian's sex tapes came out more than twenty years ago, and they didn't suddenly shrivel up and die of shame in their thirties or forties.

Even so, doing my first photos felt like a big deal. I'd sent explicit photos to men I was seeing a few times, but doing a shoot for invisible subscribers was hot on a whole other level. Just the presence of the camera turned me on, as if it was growling in my ear: *That's it. Spread your legs wider.* In truth, my first shoots were absolute amateur hour. I didn't want people to see my shitty apartment, so I hung up a sheet as a backdrop. Fucking myself with a dildo without any kind of context – no chat with the recipient, no sense of where I was in the world – was surreal, but actually hilarious. I was cackling to myself every time I ran to the camera to check the latest batch. When I uploaded them and they started to get some traction, it was the biggest high ever.

Pretty soon, I lived and breathed OnlyFans. I never went a day without posting a picture or messaging subscribers. I was so excited that guys would pay me a crazy amount of money just to talk to them. Men want to feel seen, even if they don't use their picture or their real name, so when someone subscribes to me, I'll subscribe right back to their account, slide into their DMs and ask what I should call them. Rating cocks is also huge. Men send photos of their dicks and they get a video back with a rating. Usually they just get a pre-recorded video – I've done one for each rating, like: 'Ooh, you're definitely a rock hard eight.' But if they want me to say their name, they can pay extra and I'll custom-record one, including all the reasons and ways I would like to have that cock. You can't give them too high a rating, though. Never a ten. It's just not realistic.

OnlyFans has a few different tiers. You can be a basic subscriber for just a few dollars a month and see booby photos or the odd still of a video. Then there's pay-per-view, where you pay extra to see the video or more explicit photos. There are custom options, such as the creator making a video especially for you, and then there are livestreams. These are so much fun. A few times a week (any more is frankly draining), a creator streams live to subscribers, often for hours and hours in one sitting. She'll read their messages and chat to them, and get them to tip her in order to see spicier and spicier things. She'll make sure she starts with a lot of clothes on, so that it takes longer and more tips to strip; there are all sorts of crafty ways to get dudes to pay up and stay longer. It doesn't take much. Some guys are so addicted to porn that they'd happily stay on all day, and are probably simultaneously watching another girl on another device.

Before my first livestream, I took time to create a proper set that looked cute. It was only my bedroom, but I'd removed all the clutter, bought some nice girly bedding and littered lots of sex toys around. I bought softbox studio lights, as well as cheap coloured lights from Kmart to create a bit of atmosphere, and had chosen the skimpiest lingerie I could find in Bras N Things at Pacific Fair.

Starting the stream was nerve-racking. It takes a while for people to show up and start messaging, so for the first thirty minutes I was basically talking to myself with my favourite music playing in the background, trying to be sexy with absolutely no feedback. Then guys started messaging me greetings or asking me questions, so I at least had something to work with. I've never been so grateful to see a 'Hi'.

Ding.

I got my first tip. To treat the tipper, I pushed my boobs together in my low-cut top to show him my cleavage.

Ding.

Ha! Too easy.

My clit twinged every time I heard the sound of a tip, like I was one of Pavlov's dogs. The reward system in my brain must have been lit up like the Star casino. Every time I heard a *ding* – or was that a *ker-ching*? – I got another squirt of dopamine. My ears were alert to the sound, keeping me suspended in a state of anticipation. It struck me that the *ding-ding-ding* effect wasn't a million miles from playing pokie machines. I've never been a gambler unless it's with a client's money, but I can see why people get hypnotised by that sound and the promise of what could happen next.

Ding.

Every number milestone – $50, $100, $200 – something exciting has to happen. I'm excited, too.

Ding.

I'd pull my favourite dildo towards me on the bed and tease it at the entrance of my pussy. 'You want this?' I'd ask innocently.

Ding. Ding. Ding.

'You're not getting it until we get to $1000.'

This kind of rebuke from me would usually get one or two of the viewers messaging the others, urging them to tip: 'Just a little bit. I'm putting all the money in here! Fuck you guys!' There are usually a couple taking it for the team, the poor buggers.

'Do you want me to fuck my ass or my pussy? Whoever tips $100 gets to decide.'

I started to hear those dings in my sleep.

~

Over time, I had fun getting more inventive. I'd often take my cues from gay sex workers on Twitter, because they always had the wildest, most creative ideas. One that I used to great effect was the ovipositor. This is a dildo with a hollow shaft that you push up yourself. Then you feed 'alien eggs' through the shaft, deep into your pussy, to impregnate yourself. I guess when gay guys push eggs into their asshole it's more about being invaded by an alien host and used as an incubator. Anyway, I digress. Not only do you spend a good thirty minutes inserting these diabolical eggs, one by one, but then you can spend another thirty minutes 'laying them', squatting over the floor in mock-agony as each one comes out with a distinct *pop*. Extra points if you use lots of lube that looks like alien slime. Boys really love goo.

During my first year on OnlyFans, I sent off for every kind of dildo: dildos that looked like octopus tentacles; dildos that stuck to the wall with a sucker so that you could fuck yourself hands-free; giant dildos that took almost the whole livestream session to insert, with the help of a whole bottle of lube. Side note: I once kept all my silicone sex toys in a crate too close to a window and they got melted by the sun's heat. All my subscribers' favourites were completely ruined – the anal Easter egg, the traffic cone and the foot – all fused together into one giant, wobbly frankentoy.

A couple of my videos did get flagged, including one where I'd – fairly innocently – fucked myself with a banana. I didn't know that OnlyFans had a ban on inserting objects other than sex toys. I was lucky that none of my squirting videos got banned, since – unfathomably to me – there was also a ban on gushing. Massive insertions? Sure. Orgasm? Nup.

I had my own rules: to always stop filming by 3pm and to be

completely cleaned up – showered, make-up scrubbed off, stringy lingerie swapped for a cosy onesie – and with the bedroom reset to its normal state, by 3.30pm. That was absolutely non-negotiable. Because not long after that, Baby Daddy would walk through the front door with the kids. And I needed to be 100 per cent all their mummy.

The Invisible Man

'Who's there?' I was becoming increasingly panicked. 'I know you're there. I'm going to scream.'

I sat bolt upright, scanning the room. The camera facing the bed watched me impassively.

Suddenly, the sheet jerked away in a violent movement, leaving my naked body exposed. I screamed. I hoped it looked convincing. I'd had to yank the sheet using the hand that was out of shot. This was the fifth take already.

An anonymous subscriber had been ordering custom videos from me every week for six months. They were heavily scripted and getting more and more outlandish. I was good at drama at school, but it was extremely hard to make scenes described as 'the invisible man has his way with you' look good. I should at least have won a Golden Globe for trying.

People think this story's cute. *Oh, he's just a film buff who loves Hollow Man,* they think, glossing over the non-consensual aspect of a creep coming into your bedroom. I actually had a back and forth with the subscriber about that. He wanted me to be asleep when the invisible assailant came in, but I negotiated that I'd just be chillin' in my bed, I'd feel the covers jerk away, panic, realise that a really hot invisible guy had broken in, and then I'd be up for it.

Even though these videos were pretty PG, things started to go south. I always thought there was something a little off about this customer by the way he'd give me orders, and he always had to have the videos done by an exact time on a Friday or he'd get angry. He'd message me every few hours: 'Where is it? When am I going to get it?' Maybe he had a film club he had to take them to, I don't know.

Custom videos can be the craziest part of being an OnlyFans creator. You get an appreciation for the sheer breadth of people's kinks. It's possible that the platform itself has a role to play in this splurging of imagination. As OnlyFans grew and grew, it started to prohibit certain acts, such as having sex in public, inserting objects and squirting. Well, scarcity breeds creativity. In Japan, pornographers legally have to pixelate genitals. That should have been a disaster for the porn industry there, but instead they started churning out gross-out videos such as bukkake (multiple guys coating a woman's face with cum) and gokkun (women drinking multiple guys' cum from a container). Now I think about it, the Japanese have a whole genre of invisible man porn in which a woman sits and eats her lunch while a real porn stud that she seemingly can't see jerks off onto her dumplings; or a woman reads the news on a TV set, completely 'unaware' that the male performer is jerking off all over her hair.

So custom videos became a big part of my week. Jackson would help me out with things like researching how much to charge and how best to set up a scene. He'd help me learn my lines if the guy had provided a script.

On one occasion I had to be a secret agent, with the instructions to coerce the guy into handing over some codes. We were in the middle of moving house at the time, so Jackson set up the camera in the smallest room that we hadn't unloaded boxes into yet. We drew the blinds and put a spotlight on me. I was wearing a trench coat, unbelted enough to suggest that I had nothing on underneath.

'You don't want to get me angry,' I warned the camera, my cleavage looming. 'You're not going to like me when I'm angry.'

Maybe it was overkill, but I snapped on one surgical glove. The script dictated that I get the codes, that I laugh triumphantly, and that I suffocate the guy to death. Of course that meant just putting a pillow over the camera, but you do have to be careful recording scenes like that. OnlyFans is ... *not* a fan of murder.

Even more difficult to pull off convincingly was Robot Girl. The video started with me motionless, staring straight ahead. Out of shot, Jackson played the Microsoft start-up chime, which he'd found on the internet. I came to life, speaking and moving robotically: 'What would you like me to do, master?' – that kind of business. Robot Girl became the guy's sex slave, stiltedly bending over and pulling her ass cheeks apart, obediently inserting a dildo into her pussy. Anything I could do solo without wincing, basically.

There have been a few custom video requests that I've considered and then rejected. One man wanted me to be a human ice-cream sundae. He asked me to pour chocolate sauce on my head and sprinkle nuts on top. I'm not sure if he really liked chocolate sundaes or if he was into scatological humiliation. Either way, he was only willing to pay $200 for that video and I'd have to pay a cleaner that much to wipe down the scene afterwards. Then there was the joker who wanted me to dress up as Steve Irwin and twerk on the Australian flag. I turned that down because I thought it was very disrespectful. I got my photo taken with Steve Irwin when I was a kid on a visit to Australia Zoo and I loved him way too much for such sacrilege.

My *favourite* thing to do might be SPH. Oh – that's sex worker speak for small-penis humiliation. If you've ever received an unsolicited dick pic, imagine getting paid handsomely to rip the owner to shreds. I'd make a video telling him that I wouldn't touch his little wiener with a barge pole and that no self-respecting woman would. I'd tell him that he's never been able to satisfy any of his partners, and that we've all been talking about it. I'd tell him my clit's bigger than his dick.

One guy sent me a picture of his cock and said, 'I want you to do your worst on me – be brutal,' and I wound up going way too dark on the guy. 'Why are you doing this? What *happened* to you?' I can't lie – it felt good to flip the script and ask a guy the kind of questions that guys ask me all the time. But I must have crossed the line, because this particular customer wound up blocking me.

His cock wasn't even that small, to be honest.

Do the Crab Walk

Every waking hour, when I wasn't filming or editing content, I was browsing other girls' profiles. I didn't know anyone in the industry and I needed to find my people. That's when my finger screeched to a halt on Honey Brooks.

I could tell we had a similar hard work ethic: this girl posted consistently and had no qualms about using the media to promote her brand by offering to lift the lid on sex work – something tabloid readers had a voracious curiosity about. I had noticed that sex workers would be written about respectfully in the media, so long as they gave good quotes. So while my bi side was excited to meet this busty woman with long blonde hair, full lips and a body firm from so much fucking, I was equally excited by her business mindset and what I could learn from her.

Like me, Honey had started doing OnlyFans solo. Then her husband, Hank, joined in, which progressed to Honey doing collabs with women while Frank filmed. Like me, they've got kids. They've always been open about that and about the better lifestyle they're able to provide their children – another thing the media seemed to present positively in articles about them.

Honey lived in Victoria, but when I contacted her she happened to be on the Gold Coast, which meant I had days to lock it in. Happily, she was keen. On the video call the day before our collab, Honey was lovely. She presented a menu of sexual activities, suggesting that we kiss, eat each other out, fuck each other with a strap-on and then present the pièce de résistance to our viewers: a double-ended dildo. She'd book an Airbnb. All I had to do was show up. Mmm. Easy, right?

Despite Honey's cheerfulness, I spent the night fretting. I worried about how I'd smell and taste – somehow that seemed more of an issue to me when it was a woman who would be going down on me, as if she would be privately ranking the pair of us in the yummy stakes. But I was also worried about that double-ended dildo. She'd shown me the one she'd bought and it was huge. How the hell was I supposed to insert it? I pictured myself backing onto it with the beep-beep-beep of a reversing truck.

All I could do was make sure I was as ready as possible. I'd packed on the fake tan (a habit I've eased up on since then). Then the morning of the meet-up I shaved everything in the shower, washed and styled my hair, and packed a big bag full of baby wipes, deodorant, lingerie, bikinis and outfits. *Here goes nothing ...*

~

When I pulled up at the address in Surfers Paradise, Honey and Hank were super welcoming. Hank looks like a Hank in the best possible way: shaggy red hair and a beard; lumberjack, strongman vibes. They're both country folk. Honey sometimes rocks an Akubra and cowboy boots, when she's not naked. Honey's the boss; Hank's a chill guy who's ready to help out however he can.

They gave me a tour of the luxe Airbnb. There was even an outdoor bath, which was perfect. Generally before you shoot a video you get some stills for the socials while you look nice and fresh. We filled that bath with water mixed with milk that Honey had brought – I'm telling you, this girl is always prepared – which was supposed to be vaguely suggestive of cum. Hank dropped some flowers in, and Honey and I knelt up in it and kissed, then took turns lying back with the milky water pooling between our breasts.

By the way, if you yourself run a slick-looking Airbnb, I regret to inform you that sex workers are using it to film scenes *big time*. In America, LA in particular, they're so onto it that they send you messages when you book: NO FILMING! I've been kicked out of many properties when the owners look up my name online, so now I usually get someone else to book them. But, yes, I hate to tell you: I've done some nasty shit at short-stay rentals.

After showering and drying off, we had a glass of wine each and got to know each other. My pro tip is to never have more than one glass of wine, because alcohol slows you down and makes it harder to cum. Plus, suddenly you'd rather party than get any work done.

Hank set up the video camera, the very action of which gets me hot. It's a bit like the rolling of a joint or the chopping of a line: it's all about the anticipation. What happens next is very much choreography. You kiss. You undress each other. You eat each other out, use toys, maybe scissor or use a dildo. Of course you can edit the video, but I prefer to do one take so it's more organic and the viewer knows how much you're getting into it – so much that you can't bear to lift your face from someone's pussy.

I started fingering Honey on the couch, her ass pointed towards the camera. I had long blinging nails and I was worried I'd hurt her, but I got the hang of inserting my fingers gently and angling inwards so I wouldn't scrape her. The excitement of being so brazen on video was as much a turn-on as being eaten out by a woman I'd only met one hour earlier. It wasn't hard for me to orgasm, knowing that my freshly shaved pussy was having its close-up. I opened my eyes to see Honey doing up the buckle of a black strap-on. I managed not to laugh. It looked so obscene, bobbing up and down beneath a giant pair of tits.

'Are you ready to take this dick?' she demanded. I was. I was so wet there was no need for any lube.

'You like that?' she asked, slapping my ass. 'Are you going to take that like a little slut?'

'I'm getting so close,' I told her, with what I hoped was a convincing gasp.

'Do you wanna cum for me?'

I writhed and moaned, and she pulled the black cock out of me.

'Come and taste your pussy, baby,' she purred, hovering her hips at my mouth so I could suck the cock. *Mmm, silicone.* Then she kissed me, hungrily.

As it would be rude not to return the favour, I strapped on the cock and Honey rode me, reverse cowgirl, squealing with delight. Then I fucked her missionary, old-school, and squeezed her breasts. Cum, cum. Kiss, kiss. Quick break: to neck some sports drinks and do a make-up touch-up.

There was no avoiding it: it was time for the double-ended dildo. I was concerned about trying to look hot on camera when I actually had to crab walk onto this motherfucking thing. If that was even how you did it. I mean, was Honey going to laugh at me if I tried to impale myself on it in totally the wrong way, like a complete amateur? Maybe she knew I was a newb, because she pushed one end firmly into my pussy first, before she scooted onto the other and settled in. There was a hilarious moment when it popped out of me when she was mid-shimmy, but we persevered, wiped our eyes and cut that bit from the scene.

Turned out, getting on this thing was only half the challenge. You then have to fuck yourselves with exactly the same momentum, because if you get out of sync it looks super awkward. And don't even get me started on doing it doggy style, where you both have to back onto it. Hank had to intervene and help us with that position, made even more difficult by the fact that we were losing our minds from laughing.

I left the Airbnb sore from fucking and laughing. There's nothing like trauma bonding to bring you close to someone, fast. Honey and I may not have filmed a collab for a while after that, but we'll always have that double-ended dildo.

The Surgeon

Daniel sent me a list of demands. My fingernails must be clean. My toenails must be painted white. My pussy must be completely waxed smooth with no landing strip – that's the very early nineties style of having a trimmed rectangle of pubic hair running down to your clit. It was a dead giveaway of how long he'd been seeing sex workers.

For a while I'd been considering going full service, but before I even got around to putting my adverts up on sites, Daniel became my first client after a sex worker he was seeing told me he'd taken a fancy to me. This guy was a brain surgeon and a bit odd, she messaged me, but look, he'd pay me $2500 an hour.

My grip tightened on my phone: *$2500 an hour*? That was beyond my expectations. The things I could do. The skincare products I could buy.

With our numbers duly exchanged, Daniel sent me a screenshot of a photo he liked of me in which I was wearing a Sailor Moon cosplay outfit. This manga cartoon character dresses like the traditional Japanese schoolgirl with a blue-and-white sailor shirt topped by a big red bow, and a butt-scraping blue mini skirt. My version was pink. Knowing that Daniel was a foot guy, I paired it with pink high-heeled pleasers, the kind strippers wear. Personally, I hate high heels – on me, anyway. I like to be comfortable, so I get around in runners or flats for bookings, unless it's specifically requested that I wear heels. And, for that reason, I've never got the hang of walking in them.

I drove to his address in bare feet, then wedged my toes into these giant-ass pleasers, swinging my legs out of my car and almost immediately stacking it. I hadn't been able to park directly outside of his apartment, and I cursed Kayla of thirty minutes ago for not having the foresight to pack runners, too. Finally, I made it to his gate, having only been stared at by a couple of dog walkers and the occupants of a few cars. I buzzed, and the gate swung open.

I was met at the front door by Daniel and a woman dressed in cargo pants and a T-shirt. (Lucky her.) He introduced her as his videographer and she smiled awkwardly. I estimated her to be about my age, so maybe she was as new to the world of filmmaking as I was to sex work. Daniel was a very sexy Black man. Good-looking, early forties, reasonably fit, closely trimmed hair. He smelled faintly of cologne. We got in the elevator, along with an old couple who had come in the front door behind me. Daniel seemed in no way as embarrassed as the videographer and me. If I didn't know better I'd say he relished the idea of his neighbours knowing he was about to fuck a sex worker who was dressed like an explosion in a gelato shop.

Up in the apartment – tastefully decorated in that way that tells you absolutely nothing about a person – Daniel and I chatted on the couch while the videographer discreetly hung back. Lightly touching my cheek and stroking my hair, Daniel explained that he doesn't like watching porn – he prefers to record his own experiences. What I knew, but what he didn't say, was that he had set himself the mission of filming himself with every OnlyFans girl on the Gold Coast.

Even being new to sex work, I knew what this meant: he wanted to admire himself, and I was there to be his mirror. I'd already been getting distinct Patrick Bateman vibes. If you've seen *American Psycho*, you'll know what I mean. If you haven't, Christian Bale plays Patrick as a preening psychopath who only fucks women so that he can check himself out during the act. There's one scene in which he's slamming a sex worker from behind, staring down the lens of his own video camera and flexing his biceps. Then he moves to another woman. Her black stilettos are resting on his shoulders, but instead of gazing at her pussy he's holding eye contact with himself in the mirror. 'Don't touch the watch,' he snaps, when one of them accidentally does so.

For Daniel, filming himself was a similarly serious matter. Even though I knew he wouldn't consider uploading our videos to a porn site, given the prestige of his job, he wanted this production to look like a full-on porn shoot. The videographer – I don't think he ever actually gave me her name, so I'll call her Shelley – filmed me walking unsteadily through the front door and strolling sexily to the couch. There, I had to give a few slow turns so Daniel could run his hand up my legs and admire my ass. He kissed me sensuously, taking his time, skirting one hand to my pussy and skimming a finger over my clit. Okay, now he had my attention.

Daniel had me stand up and slowly take off my clothes. I leaned discreetly on him to step out of my panties without face-planting on the carpet. With my bare pussy now exposed, he sucked on his middle finger and slid it in. I moaned, and he finger-fucked me, brushing his thumb on my clit. I couldn't believe my luck: $2500 an hour *and* he didn't rub my clit like a drunk with a scratchie card.

Daniel led me by the hand to the bedroom, where there were even more cameras. Shelley stopped recording to let Daniel turn them on and make minor adjustments to ensure I was in focus. I felt bad for Shelley having to edit together every conceivable angle later. Laying me down, Daniel gently lapped at my pussy, making me squirm. He clearly wanted me to know he was a connoisseur, and that included taking a very refined approach to cunnilingus. After I'd cum, I told him I was desperate to suck that beautiful cock. It *was* a good-looking cock, too: consistent in colour and sturdy in structure. Both his cock and balls smelled really clean. Sterile, even. Exactly what you'd want from a surgeon, I guess, though I didn't mind a bit of manly musk.

He fucked me very precisely, in doggy, cowgirl, reverse cowgirl. I assumed we would finish in missionary, but instead he took my foot and crammed it into his mouth, sucking on it like it was the most delectable sorbet. The more of my foot I pushed in, the more animalistic noises he'd make, grunting and moaning. Finally, he came, jerking himself off over my pedicure.

~

Over the following months I saw Daniel a lot, but I didn't get to know him. He tried to come across as a romantic guy, paying me compliments, touching my face, but every now and then I'd see his true colours: the flashes of irritation and the controlling behaviour. Sometimes he'd send Shelley home before she even started recording because he was suddenly in the mood to ravish me without worrying about his best angles. I hoped that girl was getting her money. In fact, I wished I had her number so I could text her a pep talk.

Every visit, he'd get me in a new outfit. He had a whole walk-in wardrobe full of them: some still in their packets, some that had no doubt been worn by girls before me. The guy must have spent every hour he wasn't working or fucking browsing Shein for garish lingerie, costumes with chains, tassels and every kind of highly flammable fabric. I pictured him scrolling at the Macca's drive-thru on the way home from work. Although that was unlikely: someone as fastidious as Daniel was unlikely to let fast food pollute his body. Maybe he had a virtual assistant in the Philippines whose sole job it was to choose the cheapest and nastiest outfits possible.

Daniel loved watching me make myself cum, and he had an array of dildos and vibes to facilitate the job. I quickly realised that he wouldn't let himself get off until he'd seen me squirt. I'd start off modestly enough with the vibrators, but by the end I'd be using the giant Hitachi wand – a vibrator the size of an arm. It was so intense, I'd cum hard while almost scrambling to get away from the bulbous head, screaming loud enough to get that old couple turning up the volume on *A Current Affair*.

Over time, I learned that this plush pad wasn't Daniel's main home – it was just his place in the city, close to work. It blew my mind to think about how much he must earn. He was spending a fortune on me, keeping me at his beck and call, and no doubt doing the same with other girls, too.

But seeing Daniel was becoming more and more draining. On my first visit he'd made an effort to seem easygoing, but he couldn't keep up that facade. He kept wanting me to message other girls that he'd seen on OnlyFans, but who I knew didn't do full service. He was going full Epstein, trying to get me on the recruitment path, and I wasn't comfortable with it. 'If she says yes, I'll give you $500,' he'd wheedle, but that just gave me the ick. Daniel, I regretted to admit, had completely lost his shine in my eyes – him and his beautiful cock and his bedazzling $2500 an hour.

The last time I saw Daniel, he was in one of his moods right from the start, and when he saw my feet, he absolutely lost it. Knowing that he insisted on me having a white nail-polish pedicure, I'd gone for a French. Same-same, right? *Wrong.*

'What's *that*?' Daniel exploded. He was kneeling between my legs, and for the first time I noticed a slight bald patch in his buzz cut. I'd got a bit distracted, wondering if he knew about it; his yelling shocked me out of my reverie.

'What?'

He lifted my foot with such force that I nearly fell off the bed.

'This,' he spat. 'It is not white polish.'

'It's a French pedicure,' I protested. (For anyone not in the know, a French is a nude base with a clean-white tip.)

'I know it's a "French pedicure",' he said unpleasantly, mimicking a woman's voice. 'My fucking ex-wife had them, and it's *not* what I asked for.'

I made an appeasing sound. Some men expect sex workers to be able to read their minds – and it's true that we usually can – but I had assumed that his desire for white nails was a virginal thing, and a French seemed to fit that brief.

By now, I was quite clear on why Daniel's ex-wife had left him. Yes, a surgeon's salary would be very nice, thank you very much, but his mood swings and selfish behaviour were intolerable even on an hourly basis.

As I got to the door, he reiterated: 'Don't come here again like that,' in case I hadn't got the message.

It would be the first time I ghosted a client forever, but it wouldn't be the last.

BBLs and Butt Men

I was still drinking my thickshake all the way up to the gate. Seconds before I showed the woman my boarding pass, I chucked the oversized cup into the bin. I knew I'd feel bloated for the duration of the flight, but I was taking this mission very seriously.

My trip to Istanbul was a well-worn path for OnlyFans creators. That year, Turkey welcomed an estimated 1.5 million plastic-surgery tourists, who were attracted by the budget prices – much, much lower than in Australia.

For my surgery, a Brazilian butt lift, known as a BBL, I'd been given the instruction to fatten up, because the procedure takes fat from areas such as your stomach and arms and injects it into the butt. In theory this shouldn't have been an easy mission for someone who'd previously battled an eating disorder but, as ever, I wanted to be the best at whatever task I took on.

A year into doing OnlyFans I realised I needed to go the extra mile to stand out: bigger dildo insertions, better camaraderie with subscribers, wilder body enhancements. I was also thinking about getting into professional porn, and BBLs were common in that industry, but not so common in Australia – so I wanted to get ahead of the curve, if you will.

As a teenager I'd been really insecure about my hip dips, and was dreaming up the kind of surgeries that are available now before they were even a thing. I craved a Jessica Rabbit hourglass figure. I'd had a boob job after having our second child (and before I got into the industry) but I needed the butt to round it out. It would make my waist look more snatched and it meant more money would come rolling in. Butt lovers didn't give a fuck whether your booty was natural; in fact, many guys love the surgery aesthetic. The sheer volume excites them. So I knew I'd be able to charge a fortune for anal and recoup my costs in no time. It's like when you pay an expert for a consultation: their price is high for the hour because you're also paying for all the hard work that went into their current status. Just like their knowledge, my butt would carry a high surcharge.

As the plane taxied down the runway I took one last look at my phone, scrolling through inspo photos of the Clermont Twins, Saweetie, SZA and Draya Michele. I was trying to drive out the mental images of botched jobs that I'd looked at the day before: women who injected black-market silicone, or concrete, or had legit surgery that didn't take.

The night before, I'd been stressing to Jackson: 'I don't know if I want to do this!' He couldn't offer much reassurance. The fact is, people have died from this surgery. But I've always been the type of person who, if I want something, I'm gonna go get it without thinking through all the possibilities. I don't take calculated risks; I'm way more impulsive. So it wasn't until the last minute that I started freaking out about it and overanalysing everything.

And by then it was way too late.

My package deal of surgery, flights to Turkey and accommodation was $12,000. The clinic had great reviews. Suspiciously great reviews, in fact – most of which had gone up in the same week. The before and after pictures were impeccable, too. The video consultation with the doctor went well and the staff spoke good English and were very encouraging. I paid the deposit.

Sixteen hours after take-off, we touched down in Istanbul. Waiting at the baggage carousel I checked out my fellow travellers. There were a lot of dudes with dazzling white teeth and receding hairlines, clearly here to get transplants, and a lot of women in White Fox loungewear with puffy lips.

In the pick-up zone, a driver was waiting to take me to the hotel. I only had time to check in and drop off my case before we continued on to the clinic. The rush didn't make much sense since once I got there the doctor was AWOL. Nobody seemed to know what was going on, and suddenly nobody spoke English, beyond asking for my passport and the rest of the money. Where was this well-oiled machine I'd expected? I suddenly felt really fucking vulnerable.

Eventually, the message came through that we should go straight to the hospital, but once there it was the same story – no doctor. Hours had gone by and it was dark outside. I was starting to freak out. Then the driver got a call saying the doctor was at the clinic. It was a farce. We drove back and I finally got my consultation.

The first thing the doctor said was that I hadn't put on enough fat so I wasn't likely to get the results I wanted. I knew for sure I'd gained enough weight as per his earlier instructions, so this threw me. Was he already covering his ass in case things went wrong? I was driven back to the sketchy budget hotel at the airport to try to get a good night's rest before surgery the next morning. I spent most of that night lying awake, staring at the ceiling, trying to manifest the perfect booty and put the fears out of my head.

This time tomorrow, I thought, *you'll be on your way to a whole new level of content.*

~

I was lying on a gurney, covered in scribbles to indicate where the incisions should go, looking up in incomprehension at the anaesthetist. He'd asked me if I was taking any medication and when I said the contraceptive pill, he'd got really upset. But this was the first time anyone had asked me what I was taking.

'We'll go ahead and do the surgery anyway,' he eventually snapped.

There were none of the fun games you see on TikTok when he put me under – no challenge to sing a verse of a song, not even a simple counting backwards from ten. I just went out like a light until I woke up again ... mid-operation. It was every person's worst nightmare. I could feel everything that was happening, but my eyes were taped shut and I don't know if I could have moved them anyway.

With a BBL, they roughly prod metal cannulas into your stomach to suck out fat that will go in your butt. I could feel the burning sensation of the suction, but I was paralysed. I could hear the vacuum, and the doctors and nurses talking to each other in Turkish, but was unable to speak myself. Eventually I fell unconscious, before they got to the process of injecting the fat into my butt.

When I came around, I was in the most excruciating pain I've ever felt in my life. My body was in shock. I was freezing, shaking, crying, screaming. It was a waking nightmare. A nurse had to bring me a disposable container to vomit and spit blood into. They kept assuring me I was fine, but I knew I wasn't.

From my own research I knew that you're not supposed to sit or lie on your butt for six weeks because that pressure could destroy the transferred fat and the new cells that need to form. I'd prepared myself for a long stint of standing, kneeling and sleeping on my side with pillows, and yet, I'd come around from the anaesthetic to find myself lying flat on my back. The nurses said it was fine, but I knew that if the fat cells died it wouldn't be on their watch, so why would they care? I was so out of it I had to give up arguing, because at that point, I was just trying to survive.

The whole healing process was traumatic. Every time I needed the toilet I'd have to squat over the bowl or stand and use a Shewee, because I couldn't sit down. I needed regular lymphatic drainage massages because my butt was so swollen from fluid retention, and they were excruciatingly painful. When I had my first massage at the hospital, I was shocked. The nurse peeled off my garment and I looked no different to before, only swollen from the brutal surgery. It looked like they'd taken random chunks of fat out of my back, which I hadn't known they'd do. The nurse told me it would be a good year before my body settled and I could see the full results. *What?*

The next day, things weren't much better. My body was barely strong enough for me to lift my arm, and yet the nurses were manoeuvring me to get me out of bed. They wanted the room back so they could wheel in the next patient and keep that cash flowing. With every step they made me take I screamed. When they tried to feed me I'd refuse, because food made me want to vomit. Eventually they told me they were going to get me dressed and into the car back to my hotel. One of the nurses left the room, leaving me with a male who started groping my breasts as he pulled on my hoodie. He pushed his hand between my legs and kissed my neck. I'm sure he was thinking I was so groggy that I'd never remember. The moment the female nurse came back in, he stopped. Then the same thing happened when we were alone in the elevator. If he spoke English, he was pretending he didn't, and I was unable to push him away. Months later, I'd be in my kitchen preparing a snack when the experience came back to me in a rush and I burst out crying. How many times had this creep done this to women who were effectively drugged? I tried to report it to the clinic, but I never heard anything conclusive back.

Back at my hotel, I upgraded my flight to business class because I wanted to make sure I could lie on my stomach, not knowing that by that point, a lot of the damage had already been done. The fat they injected into my butt didn't stay put. It mostly died off and disappeared within a few months.

Boarding the plane, I saw that my fellow passengers were just as dazed and bruised – many with most of their faces bandaged, having had fox-eye surgery. Safe to say, no one was looking like their passport photo.

~

About a year later, I still wasn't pleased with the promised results and I went to get a revision with a surgeon in Australia. This doctor couldn't believe what I'd been through – from them sitting me on my butt straight out of surgery to the chunks taken out of my back. And those amazing before and after pictures I'd seen? They'd been stolen from the Australian surgeon's website. He told me that when fat is sucked out of the body it's supposed to be purified before its return journey into your butt – otherwise, the cells will just die. It was pretty devastating to know I'd been through all that just for the sake of a bargain, but I was very happy with the new doctor's handiwork.

My girlies, I beseech you: don't go for budget when it comes to your body. Going to Turkey was the most traumatic incident of my life, but I got away lightly because I came home alive. Ask yourself, is this really for you? Is it something you've always wanted? Or is this a trend that'll date as surely as your Juicy Couture tracksuit? I know firsthand that once you've broken the seal and had one surgery, no matter how traumatic it was, you'll always be thinking of the next thing. After my second BBL, my ass was ginormous, but I was obsessed about what I could do next. At the time I was very image-focused – especially entering this industry, where you rely on your looks for money – but there's a fine line between enhanced and obscene.

Now that the dust has settled and I no longer rely on my looks for happiness, I'm put off surgery for life. I get my lip line tattooed, but I'll never do more BBL or lip or touch my face. The risks are far too high.

A couple of years after my surgery I started going to the gym more, sick of feeling unfit and unhealthy. As is the way with exercise, I started to lose weight, and in tandem with that, I began to receive comments from people speculating that I'd had implants removed. Weird – since a BBL isn't actually implants, it's your own fat relocated. Like any fat, you lose it if you lose weight over a consistent period of time.

In the early days I'd been so scared I'd lose my butt fat that I'd checked out other surgeries that might help maintain it ... but over time I had a change of heart. Carrying around that gigantic ass wasn't easy. It was so uncomfortable to run that I'd have to hold it in place. Treadmills at the gym were absolutely out of the question; the one time I tried, it felt like I got whiplash from my own butt. I couldn't really wear skirts or jeans where there might be a big gap around the waistband, so it only really looked good in clingy dresses.

Believe it or not, I'm also now less interested in appealing to the male gaze. I'm more confident in myself, and ultimately confidence is more attractive anyway.

So while it's crazy to think that I spent around $40,000 on two BBLs, only for them to evaporate within a few years, I feel like they served their purpose and earned out. And now I'm cool to move on. My issue is that I may need a different kind of surgery to lift and fix what's left. It's crazy that this consequence isn't well known – all we ever hear about is the celebrities who got a BBL, never about the mess that's left to mop up later down the track.

So where does that leave the poor butt men? One guy – let's call him Barry – started sending me increasingly frantic messages about my butt not being up to scratch anymore, before sending one final missive to let me know he would no longer require my services.

'You're making a huge mistake,' Barry wrote, with no context whatsoever. I sent back a question mark. For ten minutes I could see he was typing. Then I received a whole essay about the tragic loss of my big fat ass.

'I know you said you're focusing on your health, which I respect, but honestly, the main reason I booked you in the first place was because of your butt. I don't mean that in a bad way. It's just the truth. It's one of the best I've seen in real life, and I've seen a lot online, but it's not the same.

I know surgery is expensive, but if that's the problem, I could actually help. I don't mind putting money towards another BBL, if that's what it takes to keep it ...'

I messaged back, asking how much he would be prepared to contribute.

His answer: $1000.

Oh, that's fantastic, Barry. Because I have another $39,000 ready to go, I just couldn't get that one extra grand to make it happen. Missing my sarcasm, he even sent me screenshots of old photo shoots I'd done to show me the goal. The dude basically gave me a whole PowerPoint presentation on why I should keep my ass.

Yes, Barry, my ass is shrinking – and so is my patience.

When Your Friends Come to the Party

They say actors should never work with children or animals. I say porn actors should never work with their friends – not if they want to keep a straight face. Sometimes, laughing till you pee can be part of the appeal for subscribers, especially if it's a livestream you're doing with a mate.

My first live show with Honey Brooks turned into a hectic pyjama party, minus the pyjamas. We'd hired an Airbnb and set up our gear: a ring light and two stands, one for my phone and one for hers, so that we could both livestream for our own accounts. That works well, because if Girl A is getting fewer tips, you can slow down the action until Girl B's fans get frustrated and go to Girl A's page to tip her. It's great cross-promotion.

We decided to fill one bedroom with balloons, which would become a favourite party trick of mine. It's basically spin the bottle with balloons. You write down sex acts on little slips of pink paper, roll up the paper and then push them into balloons, ready to pop them whenever someone tips enough. It's especially exciting for 'looners' – people with a balloon fetish – but it's not specifically for them. It's all about keeping the dopamine dripping, baby. If there are prizes involved, the viewer turns into a gambler, hell-bent on winning.

Honey and I had bought different coloured balloons for different tiers of prizes. If we got up to $100 in tips we'd pop a pink balloon. The instruction inside might be: 'Take off your tops'. At $200? Another pink balloon: 'Get naked', 'Kiss' or 'Touch boobs'. If all the tips were coming from one guy we'd reward him by writing his name on our butts. Once we got to $500 we were upping the ante with red balloons, which could contain instructions such as 'Finger fuck' or 'Insert anal beads'. Something about the whole popping process got the guys in as much of a frenzy as it did us. I mean, I don't know if they were squealing in their mum's basement, but we were making a lot of noise.

At one point, we popped the balloon for 'Use a dildo'. It was one of those transparent, flexible dongs that always looked obscene if you waved it around. So I did a bit of that and I was about to push it into Honey's pussy when I spotted a huge bug trapped inside it, forever preserved in a massive glittery phallus. The idea that we were about to have a threesome with this bug made us scream so much it was hard to carry on.

What is it they say? Play stupid games, get stupid prizes.

I'd go on to do livestream sex shows with my friend Girthmaster – so called because of his wine-bottle-thick cock. We'd use balloons or a homemade wheel of fortune, with prizes such as 'Blow job' or 'Titty fucking' or 'Rim'. Jackson would make funny teaser posts in the days before the session – like our Christmas special, where Girthy was naughty Santa and I was pictured with his massive cock crammed in my mouth. We were always on the lookout for new ideas to keep the viewers amused. I saw one livestream where a girl was impaled on a fucking machine, with another girl controlling the speed and licking her pussy. They'd stop the machine whenever the tips slowed down and just talk shit until the money came in. More than anything else, they looked like they were having fun.

It's when you have a booking with a client that working with a friend can get problematic. Do you have a bestie who you almost have a secret language with? That you only have to look at to lose your shit laughing? Then imagine locking eyes with them over someone's saggy ball sack.

Eden Lux is my ride or die. When I first met her to do a collab, we fucked before we'd even set up the camera. So unprofessional. She's a hot, ripped little cookie, who tears around the GC on her motorbike, recording the reactions of guys gawking at her butt bouncing up and down on the seat in tight leggings. Unfortunately, I became so tight with her that we just couldn't take each other – or sex – seriously anymore. She'd moved to the Gold Coast from Canada, and neither of us had family in Australia, so we became each other's family. A dysfunctional family, for sure, but then, whose isn't?

We wound up living together after she left her deadbeat boyfriend, and got so close that we went on a trip to the States together to hustle for new collabs and clients. One guy wanted to book me, but I'd looked up where he was staying and it was this dingy motel with horror movie vibes. So I told him I'd only take the booking if he made it a threesome and paid for Eden too: 'You'll love her, she's super fit, she's a squirter like me,' et cetera. As it turned out, the guy was fine – nothing too weird or creepy – but from the moment I had to settle on the bed and kiss Eden, I started laughing.

It turns out guys don't find laughing cute IRL like they do on livestreams, because they're convinced you're laughing at *them*. I tried everything I could not to laugh. I crammed his little cock in my mouth and let the tears stream down my face as though it was choking me, but the way he kept saying, 'Yeah, you love this dick' completely set Eden off. She had nowhere to hide, as she was lying back working on her pussy with a vibrator.

'Something funny, huh?' he said sourly. 'Get on your hands and knees.'

I moved into doggy so he could fuck me from behind, but because he had me hovering over Eden, the hilarity just continued. Every time he drove into me I made a face at her that he couldn't see.

'Can you *stop*,' she hissed, barely able to breathe from laughing. When he switched and started railing her from behind, I told her to 'take it, you little bitch' before he could even get the chance.

Ah, Eden. We shouldn't be allowed out in public. Or booked for privates.

Pathway to Porn

I was such a curious kid, always seeking out things that seemed illicit and exciting. From a very young age I loved looking at the bodies in medical books, studying all the parts that were usually covered up. I even found some random pictures of women in bikinis in the *Guinness World Records* books we had at home.

It was completely by accident that I first stumbled on porn. When I was eight I was watching a horror movie called *FeardotCom* with my older siblings. The premise was that if you visited the titular website, you would die – a bit like *The Ring*, but with a URL instead of the telephone. So *of course* I used my mum's computer to look up that website afterwards. Some prankster had got hold of the domain and had uploaded porn. Mind: blown.

From then on, I was off. Titillating myself became an addiction, and I quickly learned to ramp up the naughtiness each time to satisfy what my brain was craving. These were the days of dial-up internet, and I would have racked up some massive bills looking at porn that

I'm sure my brother wound up getting the blame for. I was really trying to get my head around sex – what went where and in what order, and what it might feel like for both men and women. The ladies were always so glamorous and immaculately made up, and were often sneering or growling, like femmes fatales. They seemed powerful and alluring to me, as if they held the keys to some kingdom the rest of us had no idea about.

There was an early influencer called Tila Tequila who had a show called *A Shot at Love with Tila Tequila*, in which both men and women competed for her affection. She had a mainstream TV career but then moved into porn. Thirteen-year-old me was fascinated by that, because usually you hear about the pathway the other way around: adult performers trying to become 'legit' through mainstream TV. It was food for thought.

You could say I was exploring my primal instincts, which is my shonky segue into how I started acting in porn movies for the first time. The first guy I worked with was Dale Egan, aka Primal Instincts. Like me, Dale had permanently landed on the Gold Coast, where he had a big open-plan pad with lots of natural light, perfect for filming. His schtick was having multiple women in a scene, with him as the befuddled guy who decides he'd better just get on with it. His videos had the barest hint of a plot: 'I was in the wrong hotel room'; 'Pool cleaning at the sorority house'; 'Plumber's lucky day'; 'Delivering room service'; 'Walking in on girls' movie night'; 'Electrician didn't expect the extra leak' ... you get the idea.

If I'm honest, I thought he'd be a Gold Coast douchebag, because he has the bro look that's popular up here: muscly physique, high fade, stubble, tattooed sleeves. A friend had recruited me for the video shoot but I nearly cancelled on the day, before deciding I'd better just grit my teeth and do it so that my reputation didn't take a hit.

The shoot turned out to be with three other girls, one of whom I knew – but she has since fallen off the face of the earth, as is so often the way with OnlyFans girls. You probably don't know their real name so you'll never be able to track them down again. We'd arranged to turn up wearing casual beachwear, and I absolutely plastered myself with fake tan, which I was really into at the time. I found an eye-popping orange bikini top and paired it with tiny denim shorts. You couldn't miss me.

Dale greeted us warmly and served us all energy drinks on ice while we touched up our make-up in his bathroom, subtly jostling for the best light. It was a really laidback vibe: literally just Dale and a nervous-looking videographer, and us girls. Dale introduced the videographer as Paul and said he was testing the guy out to see if he liked the gig. Paul smiled sweatily and shuffled backwards into the shadows.

The plot called for us to let ourselves into Dale's apartment – now reimagined as a holiday home – only to find him chilling on the sofa, which means the place had been double-booked. Oh no! What to do? Cue sex.

When Paul called 'action', we all bounced through the front door, wheeling our little suitcases behind us. One girl did most of the acting, so all the rest of us had to do was agree with her if she looked at us.

'Do you think we could all fit on this couch?' Dale was saying, looking flummoxed. 'Maybe we could try.'

'Maybe we could!' *Giggle.*

Once the dialogue stopped and the sex began, I sprang into action. I know my best angles and I wanted to make sure I bagged the positions that provided them. First stop: Dale's cock in my mouth. My TikTok handle – Blue Eyed Kayla Jade – only came about because I'd been kicked off the platform so many times that I had to come up with yet another name; but all the same, I do use eye contact to devastating effect when I'm giving head. From the camera's point of view there are big blue eyes, pink lips wrapped around a dick and my boobs filling the frame. Can't lose.

Sometimes there'll have to be a lot of cuts in the final edit because someone makes everyone else laugh, but I prefer to power right through for more authenticity. The exception is when you're hitting a technical pose like a double penetration, where it can look a bit awkward in the set-up.

The three of us girls tag-teamed Dale through his paces and then the scene ended with the agreement that we could all definitely fit on that couch if we tried. I should actually give a shout-out to that couch. For some bizarre reason, Dale saw fit to buy this beautiful big white leather couch – a couch completely incompatible with shooting porn, or even with the Gold Coast. Since that first scene I've left so many fake tan ass and boob prints on it. To this day, he tells me that he had to get the cleaners overtime whenever we shot a scene, because of the tan, the squirting, the baby oil. But, I mean, who buys a white couch? RIP.

We were going to shoot some behind-the-scenes footage, but the videographer bailed. Paul had been looking peaky and he said he was actually going to be sick. I will admit that a big load of cum, sweat, squirt and the pong of fake tan is a pungent mix, but seriously – he should try shooting a multi-guy scene and then get back to me.

~

By the time summer rolled around that year, I'd managed to form a tight crew of Gold Coast girlies who would all help a sister out with referrals and opportunities. If someone was shooting a scene we'd check in with them afterwards and make sure they were okay and share tips on staying safe, checking references, that kind of business. It all went in the group chat.

Later, two of us moved into full-service sex work at the same time and we continued being that safety net for each other: 'I'm going to be at this hotel tonight with this person. If you don't hear from me by this time, ring me.' We'd always debrief after a booking and totally roast the guy. It helps to vent with someone who gets it, because even if you've had a rough time you wind up turning it into comedy gold and blowing your ring laughing. It was those no-holds-barred phone calls that formed the basis of my TikTok posts and my confessional podcast. I wanted the public to feel like they were literally debriefing with me, one on one.

Knowing so many girls would be on set that first day with Dale meant I felt safe working with him, but actually, as I got to know him, I realised he was a true diamond in the industry. He was always generous with his contacts and advice, having been around for a few years. I very nearly had a horrible sliding doors moment when I was about to work with another male creator. Dale warned me that he had heard bad things about this guy, so I pulled the plug – and later I heard way more sordid tales to back up this guy being bad news. Everything could have gone south, but instead, thanks to people like Dale, my start in the industry was a very positive one.

My other main compadre in this industry is Girthmaster, the man with Australia's biggest appendage – although he's now moved to LA to give the big boys out there a run for their money. You'd like Ben.

My mum loves him. Jackson loves him. In fact, he and Jackson are very similar in humour and temperament.

The first time I met Ben, as his mother still calls him, I drove to his little apartment in Brisbane. I was wondering what I'd been thinking, agreeing to shoot with a guy with a schlong the width of a wine bottle, but he was so professional. Ben earnestly sat me down and talked about the importance of listing my dos and don'ts and of making sure there were consent forms. I mistook him for being very serious, but I couldn't have been more wrong.

After we finished our scene I invited him to Sexpo – a sex industry conference that was on in the city – and it turned into a wild night that sealed our bond. We bumped into one of my earliest fanboys, who had come up from Melbourne. This guy had sent me birthday and Christmas presents every single year since I started on OnlyFans. He couldn't afford to pay for any of my services, but I did want to show him a good time, so Ben and I wound up taking him to the Sexpo afterparty. We encouraged girls to give him lap dance after lap dance as we drank sambuca shots. I couldn't tell you what time the fanboy left, but I do know that he left a very happy man.

Ben's a kind-hearted guy. He probably gets as many annoying messages from guys as I do, only in his case it's all dudes wanting to get into the industry to fuck as many women as possible, trying to get him to share his contacts. As he warns them, a male performer has to be able to get hard instantly, stay hard all day and pop on call. I can vouch that most men will cum in the first twenty minutes and not be able to get hard again, and not even the agony of knowing that they've paid for four hours will persuade their cock to behave itself.

In all of our collabs, Ben and I had the kind of fun that frequently crossed over into idiocy. Whenever I gave him head I'd blow bubbles of spit and cum, and go cross-eyed, to make him laugh. Sometimes we'd film with another girl, sometimes with another guy – like the time we shot with Dale and the two of them double-penetrated me. It may only have been twenty minutes, but it was twenty minutes of near-death experience. Ya girl needed a medal after that one.

One memorable day, Ben and I were filming a foursome at a hotel with two other girls and we got kicked out. It was a beautiful boutique hotel in Brisbane, built around a pool. Before we started, we shot some reels of us getting sexy in our lingerie. Obviously that content is intended for posting on socials once the final video is edited, to drive people to buy it, but one of the girls got excited and posted a reel right then and there, even tagging the hotel. Of course, the rest of us didn't know this. We were mid-scene, two of us girls giving Ben a blowjob, when there was a knock on the door. A man told us we had to leave immediately because we were filming content. We denied it, but we didn't put up much of a fight. It was so awkward, packing our bags and doing the walk of shame through the lobby. Within a few hours I received an email, basically a legal notice, saying I should never go back and I should not put the video online. I didn't answer that one. I did go back, though. And the video got a lot of tips.

Ben earned enough money with his massive schlong – and his good attitude – that he could buy his mother a house. That was a dream he'd been manifesting since he was a fifteen-year-old relying on Centrelink payments. I imagine it eased his mother's pain of finding out her son was known worldwide as Girthmaster. Ben constantly lectured me to be more frugal with my money and I credit him with setting me on that path.

I was so sad when Ben moved to LA. Thankfully I still have his replica cock, which I have, of course, put through its paces as video content. Ben wants to transition to the mainstream and I'm sure he will. I keep telling him that's not how Tila Tequila did it, but he doesn't listen.

The Dark Side of OnlyFans

If you're going to be a sex worker on the internet, you have to be prepared for the worst. First and foremost, you cannot expect to stay under the radar. Some subscribers will record their screens and upload the results to porn sites – I guess as a public service to their fellow tuggers who don't want to pay. For that reason, if I do a video call with a guy, I do it on Snapchat, because that platform tells you if someone is recording or screenshotting – although someone could just film the Snapchat with another phone if they wanted to. Where there's a will there's a way.

You may also get doxed. If someone in your real life gets wind that you're on a platform such as OnlyFans, they may subscribe purely to expose you. One of Jackson's extended family members, a man in his forties, did that to me, sending my pictures to the family group chat to show what kind of girl I was. The same thing famously happened in the ninth season of *Married at First Sight Australia*, when a contestant circulated a nude of one of her co-stars in order to shame her. That poisonous little game wound up with both women being criticised in the national media. And as for Jackson's relative? After I bawled him out the next time I saw him, neither of us spoke to him again. Everyone hates a dobber.

Way worse than that was the doxing of my kids. By the time I'd been on OnlyFans for three years, and working as a full-service sex worker for two years, I had accumulated around 2 million followers. I had to become thick-skinned enough to deal with the fact that there would be snarky forum threads about me and lies told, but then the worst happened: it seemed that certain people on mummy message boards had figured out that I had children, and thought that it was their story to tell.

Overnight, it was like a pigeon had been let loose in the house: total chaos. The 'news' that I had children had spread to other gossip groups. The comments were full of people asking what my kids looked like, their ages, and even asking for photos, like my children were playing cards to be traded. Even worse were the dramatic theories people were coming up with. It's wild that people act like true-crime internet sleuths, intent on busting some mystery, when actually all they're doing is speculating and trying to expose the identity of actual children. Round of applause to you. Honestly, they were sharing information that was literally ridiculous.

Exhibit one: that I was a bad mother because I didn't parade my kids in any of my daily videos, which must mean I was neglecting them.

Exhibit two: that I didn't have custody of my kids, or they'd been taken away.

I wound up launching my podcast, *Storytime With Kayla Jade*, early so I could address the nonsense and lay the more outlandish rumours to rest. But the truth was, it was heart-wrenching. I'm all about women supporting women, so to see that women were putting their fucking tea in front of children's safety really broke me. I love women. I have so many beautiful interactions through my platform and I'm always thinking of the women who follow me whenever I post: what do they want to know about sex work? What heads-up about new products can I give them? How much can I show them about my life?

It's become a real problem that people with big followings on TikTok and Instagram are targeted by bullies in snark groups. I've watched with interest as some influencers have decided to push back and take legal action, working towards outing the people who are libelling them.

Then there are the stalkers. Many sex workers I know have had people showing up at their house. They're always looking over their shoulder and expecting the worst. Sometimes they have to move house. Like, repeatedly. I heard one crazy story about a man who zoomed in on a creator's photo to read the name on her dog's collar. He already knew what suburb of his city she lived in because he recognised a bar that she'd once posted a photo of herself in. He rang every vet in that suburb and told them he needed to bring in his dog, giving them the name he'd seen on the collar. He'd say, 'Is this where my girlfriend usually brings him? She usually takes care of the vet stuff.' Once he'd found the vet, there wasn't much he could do with the information, short of staking out the clinic for months, but he did triumphantly message the creator to let her know he'd figured out where she lived and what her surname was.

Guys like that will put the same kind of dedication into harassing women as I did making myself a success on the same platform. But their brand of hyperfocus is so very dark.

Feeder Boy

The desire to control another person can take many different forms. It's something that occurred to me as I picked biscuit crumbs out of my cleavage. An anonymous subscriber had ordered a custom video of me scoffing a whole packet of Tim Tams, followed by a tub of ice cream.

At first, his intent to turn me into human foie gras just seemed funny. Okay, so as well as paying me $500 for a custom video, you're also going to cover the expenses of my supermarket run? Sure, boy! Sign me up. But this guy was a 'feeder', someone who gets off on watching women gorge themselves to the point of discomfort. And trust me, there was nothing overtly sexual about these videos.

Feeder Boy appeared out of nowhere and ordered a rapid spurt of videos and photos. Sometimes he'd have me saying, 'Mmm, I *lovvvve* stuffing myself', with my mouth full and cheeks bulging. Sometimes he'd want me to mic myself up around my stomach, to catch the audio of me having just drunk a whole thickshake. I'd wobble my belly around to try to make a sloshing noise.

Then there was the weight-gain progression that he'd want me to log. As well as photos of me pushing my belly out, which I'd take from a wily angle to make myself look bigger, I'd make a video weighing myself every morning. I'd add a few easy kilos by hiding a dumbbell behind my feet, out of shot.

But I started to wonder if Feeder Boy was a risky client. What was his end goal? To keep me to himself, or ruin my earning spree by making me fatter? I was relieved when he simply disappeared after a few months of frenzied contact. I never learned what his motivation was. For all I know, he was a girl from my old high school, trying to plump me up for a laugh.

Actually, a lot of people *do* like to watch me eat. When I make martinis for my TikTok videos, I'll add weird ingredients such as blue cheese – things that are viscerally smelly even if you're on the other side of the screen. Or I'll cram a burger, dripping with cheese and sauce, into my mouth. The people who like these videos probably aren't feeders or 'chubby chasers'; I think there's just an appreciation for a perfectly made-up girl getting stuck in and messy. It's a bit like when an immaculate-looking adult movie star gobbles a big cock until her mascara runs.

There's also a South Korean trend called mukbang, which has spread across social media worldwide, picked up by all kinds of content creators. This is where people film themselves stuffing themselves with huge quantities of food. They talk to the camera at the same time, so there are a lot of wet mouth sounds. Some people can't stand that, but the noise does appeal to people who are into that kind of autonomous sensory meridian response (ASMR). So with this in mind, when I eat on camera I'll lick the sauce from my blinging nails, occasionally also using my talons to scoop up food, caviar spoon–style. Hey – your ick is someone else's yum.

In my opinion, getting paid for these videos is a dangerous game for anyone who's ever had an eating disorder. Either they let themselves become obese (unthinkable) or they make themselves vomit afterwards. The only reason I was safe was that I completely, finally, overcame my own eating disorder when I was pregnant with my first child. There was no way I was going to risk the health of my baby, so for the first time my preservation instinct was stronger than my death wish.

When my anorexic behaviour began, at fifteen years old, various conditions had formed a perfect storm. Having ADHD – back then, undiagnosed – meant I was prone to obsession, and I'd find one thing to hyperfocus on after another. Looking back, the early 2010s were ripe for giving girls eating disorders. Early fitness influencers such as Kayla Itsines and Ashy Bines were launching bikini body challenges left, right and centre. I was obsessed with YouTube videos of super-slim women discussing what they ate in a day. Orthorexia – obsession with healthy eating: think #cleaneating #fitspo #thinspiration – was huge, and that's where it started with me.

Added to that, my parents had just split up. Throughout my life I'd never seen any affection between them, so it wasn't a huge surprise. Mum and I were close, but as she'd just become a single parent, she wasn't able to supervise me as closely. Mum converted the garage at her new place into a granny flat for me, with its own kitchen and bathroom, which meant I was able to hide food, or lie and say I'd already eaten on the way home from school. And the number of jumping jacks and mountain climbers going on behind my door was insane.

I'd also started seeing James, who at thirty was much older than me. I had such a thing for older men. They were like my fetish: something that I actively pursued, like I was the hunter and they were the prey, and they would be unable to resist me because I was so young and corruptible.

The relationship quickly morphed from hot to controlling to violent. Being with James made me feel so insecure. He'd put me down in front of our group and flirt with other girls. It hadn't even occurred to me that him having a girlfriend fifteen years his junior, not even of legal age, made him a major creep and, technically, a sex offender. But I was determined to show I could handle whatever adult life could throw at me. He and the new crowd I was hanging out with were into stimulants and party drugs, which staved off hunger cravings and made it easier for my eating disorder to hide in plain sight.

When James and I eventually broke up, I spiralled. He'd cheated on me, and the loss of control I felt as a result made me want to ramp up the grip I could hold over my body. I took long hikes in the bush surrounding Mum's place and increased my exercise to around eight hours a day, including going to the gym and high-cardio HIIT classes. I discovered online forums where girls obsessed over their eating disorders like they were in a cult. I was becoming more and more isolated from the real world. I avoided friends because they'd worriedly comment on how thin I was. New boyfriends were off the menu because losing so much weight meant I had zero libido, and when I did try, sex was super uncomfortable.

Denial is such a weird thing. I'd developed a jaundiced tone to my skin and soft down on my body – both signs of an eating disorder – but the way I saw it, 'succeeding' at only eating a minimal amount of food was on par with getting A grades at school: it showed I had discipline and willpower, which couldn't possibly be a bad thing. And yet anorexia had taken over every moment of my life. On one family holiday, I'd get up at four in the morning, do a massive workout and then go to the chemist to buy laxatives. My mum was trying to confront me, and she roped in my brother and sister, too, but trust me: you can't tell a person with ADHD what to do. If they were watching me at a food court or restaurant, I just made sure that I ordered the smallest, healthiest meal possible, and then I'd excuse myself to the bathroom and puke it back up. This was new, but necessary.

Back at home, the situation was taken out of my hands when I collapsed one day. My electrolyte levels had dropped so low that I'd been getting palpitions and could feel my heart skipping beats. Freaked out, I called for my mum and she took me to the doctor. He took one look at me and sent me to the emergency department. Within the hour, I was hooked up to an ECG, a saline drip and a feeding tube.

For the first time, my behaviour was given a name: anorexia. Despite the evidence, I was shocked, because I really hadn't thought it was a problem – not when every other girl I met online, on those forums, was doing the exact same things as me. But when I admitted to the doctor that I hadn't had my period for a couple of years, I could see the horror on Mum's face.

'The way you were going, your heart could have cut out even walking to the letterbox,' the doctor told me sternly.

I spent nearly a month in hospital – first in the cardiac ward, then the mental health ward, which I was outraged about. 'Why am I on the mental health ward?' I demanded. 'I'm just thin!'

I met some of the most beautiful souls on that ward, but also some of the most desperately mentally ill people. A weird thing happens when you put a bunch of girls with eating disorders together: in therapy we would deliberately talk about our experiences in a way that allowed us to thrillingly relive them, triggering the fuck out of each other. We were all damaged girls, the kind who bad men like to prey on. Predatory men can sniff out a person with low self-esteem a mile off. Just think of the feeders and their desire for control. In extreme cases – be it within a real relationship or a transactional relationship – they want a woman to become incapacitated, bedbound or even dead.

At the hospital, we all had regular individual appointments with a dietician called Tanya. To this day I can't figure out why anyone in management thought it was a good idea for this woman to work there, because she was a stone-cold bitch. Put it like this: if ever a client wants me to role-play being mean, I channel Tanya. She talked about our bodies in a way that's 101 what you're not supposed to do with somebody who has an eating disorder. 'You've got broad shoulders, so with that kind of body type you shouldn't be this thin.' Or: 'You're looking *so* much healthier now.'

A little under a month later, once I'd reached a certain weight, I was committed under the *Mental Health Act* to an eating disorder clinic in Wellington for five months. It was a bit like being in prison in that you got to learn how to pull off all kinds of tricks. Everyone there had their own methods of conning people into thinking they were eating. You couldn't win, though, because you were weighed every morning; so, while we were there, at least, we really did have to put on weight. It was stressful sitting down to eat with a bunch of girls with eating disorders, because being competitive perfectionists, we were always silently appraising each other. Some were anorexic, some bulimic, some binge eaters and some all three. Other than that one family holiday, I had never really got into purging. But the girls at the clinic would talk about it and I thought, *Hmm, okay. I need to be doing that, too.*

When I was deemed well enough to leave, I didn't become an

outpatient because Palmerston North was too far away to travel, so I was left to my own devices. In any given food-related situation, I was expending huge energy on figuring out how I could get out of eating. I can't lie – coming up with devious plans gave me a lot of satisfaction. By then I was bulimic, rather than anorexic. Over time I developed what's called sialadenosis: chipmunk cheeks and swollen salivary glands from puking.

Mum was hovering around me more than usual at mealtimes, but she assumed I was better because they'd released me. At seventeen I was also practically a full-grown adult, so there was only so much she could do. As for Dad, he didn't say anything about it, which was his modus operandi. He's from that generation where you just squash down any trauma and develop a stiff upper lip. He didn't understand my eating disorder and he didn't recognise it as a mental health problem. I kind of got that. I was developing an allergy to talking to psychiatrists. Every day during my stay at the clinic I had an appointment to see one, but I struggled to open up to people I didn't know. That might seem ironic for someone who now chronically overshares in a podcast and on TikTok, but I get to control the narrative and carefully curate what I put out there. Control, control, control; it's still all about control.

I still binge-eat on occasion if I'm stressed, but I could never see myself becoming anorexic again or picture myself putting my fingers down my throat. When clients take me out to fancy restaurants, I'll absolutely order the best, often five courses, and not feel guilty.

At home, I'm the master of the roast. I'll spend all day cooking one the way my grandmother used to do; it's my way of nurturing the people I love, and of calming myself through something meditative.

If there's one thing I have retained from my eating disorder days, though, it's my ability to keep secrets. That's one reason my clients love me. When I need to be, I'm a vault.

Do You Shein?

I know it can't be true, but it feels like I'm single-handedly keeping Shein afloat with my role-play request wardrobe. Every week brings an insane new costume demand from my subscribers and clients, either for custom videos or for real-life freakery. The most common orders are for the gym bunny/girl in tight yoga wear look, and the secretary.

One secretary booking in particular was weird. I met the guy at the hotel and he presented me with wine and chocolates. For the first hour, Michael told me about how much he liked his real PA, but said he was prevented from acting on his feelings because of professional etiquette and the uneven power dynamic. I had to feel sorry for him, because this guy clearly had it bad – he'd even been considering looking for another job because he couldn't stop fantasising about her. He was hoping he could get the obsession out of his system by booking me: a bit like when you have a song stuck in your head you just have to listen to something else to override it.

Michael wound up extending the booking for another hour because he talked all through the allotted time, and had paid for my hair and outfit, too – not your stereotypical tight skirt and low-cut blouse secretary costume, but a tasteful wrap dress: the kind his real PA liked to wear. He wound up spending around $5000 on this experiment.

The sex was pretty good. He took it slow. Every now and then he called out her name and I made sure to moan. Then, as he was finishing – the final shudders and twitches – he told me he loved me. Or told her he loved her. Either way, it was awkward; like, what am I supposed to say? I couldn't bring myself to say 'I love you' back in case it seeded some new obsession in him, so I just said, 'Thank you.'

By the way, if you're looking for office-related inspiration, you could check out the 2002 film *Secretary*, with James Spader as a creepy, dominant lawyer, and Maggie Gyllenhaal as his submissive secretary who's always up for a spanking over the desk. More recently, in 2024, *Babygirl* tackled the same kind of subject but flipped it – Nicole Kidman plays the powerful boss who is drawn into a BDSM relationship with her male intern, played by Harris Dickinson. I saw it at the cinema and laughed all the way through it, but maybe that's just me.

The sexy psychologist is a close cousin of this idea. I've got a guy friend whose new girlfriend enticed him to do role-play. She's an actual psychologist and she asked him to play the patient. She dressed up in high heels and a pencil skirt, with lots of make-up, so he was pretty excited and impatient to get through the session. To his dismay, she spent almost a full hour quizzing him on his relationship patterns and was digging for information on his previous girlfriends. At the end she said, 'Unfortunately I don't think I can take you on as a client because I'm very sexually attracted to you,' and they had sex – but he was pretty freaked out by that point.

If you love dress-ups, I encourage you to take up pole dancing, because, I swear, the girls entering the regular routine nights in their local studios come up with the most insane ideas. Otherwise, here are some looks to get you started:

- **Lara Croft.** (Best for: those who are comfortable with strong women.) Very easy for my babes with long dark hair. Get some tiny shorts, an army-style singlet, a leather holster and a garter. Gun optional. You can actually wear this out – minus the leather accoutrements – and then just add the garnishes once you're in private.

- **Britney Spears in '... Baby One More Time'.** (Best for: those who haven't really thought much about role-play.) It's not massively imaginative, but it's cute. Grey cardigan, school skirt, white shirt tied at the waist, hair in bunches. Maybe some over-knee socks. Done. Keep it in the back of the closet for the next time someone runs a school disco night.

- **Daphne from *Scooby Doo*.** (Best for: nerds.) When I put a picture of me dressed as Daphne on my OnlyFans, requests went through the roof. Clingy purple (or dark) dress, matching headband and neck scarf. It's a little bit flight attendant, a little bit seventies groover.

- **Uma Thurman.** (Best for: gen-Xers.) You can go for either the iconic yellow motorcycle suit from *Kill Bill* (it's got that front zip for slow reveals) or the *Pulp Fiction* vibe of a black wig, choker and winged eyeliner. Either way, guys in their forties and fifties will get a nostalgic hard-on (see also: Princess Leia as a slave girl in *Return of the Jedi*).

- **Harley Quinn.** (Best for: other girls.) Margot Robbie's *Suicide Squad* creation, with the blue and pink bunches and Daddy's Little Monster shirt is a real fave with girlies. I do wonder if women love it more than men (maybe men are put off by the baseball bat). I think guys tend to be more basic in their comic-book tastes and will take a Catwoman leather one-piece any day.

Welcome to Disneyland

Usually when a guy asks, 'You like that, baby?' he doesn't want a truthful answer. He's just getting himself off with a narcissistic monologue. At best, you are his mirror. At worst, he's hoping it hurts.

That wasn't the case with Dredd. When Dredd asked me if I liked something, the tone in his voice implied he was actually concerned – particularly as he'd have to stop rimming my asshole and pull his face out of my crack.

'I do,' I assured him. I meant it.

Dredd specialises in BBC – big black cock. He's far more chill than his name, which is a reference to his dreadlocks, suggests. He's a real favourite with size queens. Born in the Bronx, he got his start in porn in Miami, and was in his early fifties by the time we worked together. His cock is 12 or 13 inches long, depending on which production company is writing the copy. Let me tell you, though, that one inch makes quite a difference when you're psyching yourself up to take it in your ass.

As Dredd's thing is anal, if I wanted to work with a big name like him, that was what I was going to have to do – and since I'd flown all the way to LA, there was no going back now. For me, doing anal is more of a mental than physical barrier. It takes a lot of preparation, plus male performers can be a lot rougher in anal scenes to make it look really hardcore. But the truth is, if you're properly warmed up, you can accommodate way bigger cocks anally than vaginally because the sphincter is more flexible. I remember Girthmaster saying he did a scene with Joanna Angel and she couldn't fit his massive cock in her pussy, but she cheerfully said, 'That's okay – I'll get it in my ass.' And she did.

This was my first of three visits to the States with Jackson and the kids in tow. For the first part of each day I'd film as much production-house porn and as many OnlyFans collabs as I could, which freed me up to spend the rest of the day with the family, hitting up Disneyland and the other theme parks. Jackson and I are just big kids ourselves, so we loved it.

Yes, it's quite the double life, switching between porn mode and mum mode, but I've always been able to keep the two personalities very separate. People ask all the time how I can do that. Just like I have two suitcases, one for jobs and one for family time, I have two versions of myself. It helps that I firmly believe that I don't need to hold any shame around having sex, including sex on camera and sex for money. It's shame that makes people hide parts of themselves or bring out their dark side.

I did envy the extra hours that Jackson and the kids got to spend in the hotel pool, but at the same time I was beyond excited to be collecting these big-name porn performers, like notches on the bedpost of my career. The way my mind works: whatever I do, I want to excel at it. It's not necessarily healthy, but my single-mindedness and work ethic has elevated me way above the lifestyle that a girl from Palmerston North would normally be destined for.

Over at Dredd's place, he'd hired a videographer and a small hair and make-up team. For my part, I'd loaded my work suitcase with lots of little outfits, toys and lube. But, as it turned out, all I wore were white knee socks. He sat and talked to me as I got made up, and I could have listened to his voice forever; it was deep and resonant, like Morgan Freeman's. He seemed keen to get to know me, asking what kind of music I was into and what my interests were and what the Gold Coast was like. He came across as a father-figure, giving me a lot of advice, making sure I was shooting with the right people. I was quite in awe of him.

If you're working on a porn shoot, like for the major production company Brazzers, there are 2257 model release form papers to sign, a boundary checklist, and probably a talent liaison to be your advocate on set and to stop filming if things get a bit overwhelming. In our case it was an OnlyFans collab, but Dredd was still careful to go over boundaries with me and do everything above board. He asked me about anal and I said we could try it – which was fucking ballsy of me, actually, because I had not prepared at all. Luckily he had douches in his bathroom, so when I was done in the hot seat I locked myself in there and got one foot up onto the basin.

While it's nice to have a laugh and all that friendly preamble, once filming starts, the atmosphere changes very abruptly: the language goes from fun to intense, and there's a let's-do-this focus. Most of the porn videographers I've worked with have had a similar way about them: mobster accent, kinda sleazy, but also pretty warm once you get to know them. Dredd's guy was no exception – rough around the edges beforehand, but entirely focused on the job at hand once we started. That professionalism gave me comfort.

We started with me jiggling and whirling my boobs at the camera. They were looking even bigger, thanks to the contrast of my tan lines, and in the edit the videographer rendered the scene in slow-mo, so if you were a titty guy you could just get lost in the undulating motion.

Then Dredd pulled me to him, talking to me gently. He has a huge horse cock, giant and curved. It was like trying to blow a giant zucchini. My eyes were watering as he murmured his instructions on how he liked it.

'That's what I'm fucking talking about, so fucking good.'

I gingerly backed onto him in reverse cowgirl. 'You're good, you're good, come on down,' he assured me. It was like going on a rollercoaster ride. No condom, of course. People don't get turned on by seeing a sheathed dick. I've only ever caught one STI working in the industry, which is probably less than a civilian might get just hooking up with people on the apps. To shoot porn you have to get the whole battery of tests, including HIV, every two weeks. The service most performers use in LA is a really chill place. There's a hot chocolate station, a spin-the-wheel where you can win merch, and the nurses are all rad.

All the while, Dredd was like a courteous driving instructor. 'Good.' 'Very good.' It was reassuring and kinda hot. I'm more of a carrot girl than a stick girl – tell me I'm doing well, don't tell me I'm a dirty ho. For forty minutes we alternated between sucking and ass-fucking. I just focused on relaxing so I could sink my ass as far down his length as possible. I couldn't go balls deep – I'm not sure anyone has – but I wanted to at least give every other girl a run for her money.

After that scene, I cleaned up and then got straight in an Uber to Universal Studios, to meet up with the family. On the way, I called Girthmaster and debriefed with him: so fucking excited that I'd actually survived a session with Dredd's monster cock that I didn't even bother keeping my voice down. You'd better believe the Uber driver angled his mirror to check me out. Girth said I sounded like an ultramarathon runner who had just finished a race: breathless, elated, on a massive high.

'I don't know how I *did* it,' I kept saying. 'Forty minutes with Dredd. Fuck, it was *amazing*.' It was the sort of achievement you want to scream out of the window at everyone you pass, but unfortunately not everyone feels the same way about it.

Jackson had been playing nanny all day, so it's possible he was even more tired than I was, but you can't not get fired up at these theme parks. First, though, I had to line up and clear security. There was a bag check, and I realised too late that the woman was going to go through my little case in front of everybody in the queue. I swear I watched her unzip it in slow-mo. There it was: all the gear I hadn't even needed to use with Dredd. Tons of lingerie. Lube. A giant dildo. Vibes. She rummaged through it and then just zipped the case right back up again, her face unmoved. It was impressive, honestly. She motioned for me to raise my arms and patted me down, but there was no more contraband to find.

Once reunited with the fam, I refuelled with a Krusty Burger, followed by a couple of Lard Lad Donuts; I'm always starving after a scene, and TikTok does love a good 'Everything I ate at …' video. In our early days Jackson and I had bonded over *The Simpsons*, so we were excited to visit the fictional Springfield and ride the rollercoaster. Even though I was tired I made the most out of every second, checking out the Bates Motel and the set of *Jaws*. There's probably more video footage of our family at Universal Studios than there is of my on-set antics that trip.

Much later, back at the hotel, I had the usual adrenaline dump. With the kids in bed, Jackson ran me a hot bath. Being on set is like being in a boxing match: at the time you've just got to get through it, so you don't feel pain, but later it hits you like a truck. I massaged my aching perineum in the oily bubbles and languished till the water ran cold. Jackson came and sat on the toilet seat so I could tell him all about it. He gets all the details, and while he's always on high alert that I'm keeping safe, he's also just genuinely fascinated by the whole industry.

Somehow, before Dredd and I even got to upload that video to our OnlyFans accounts, it was leaked. I was so pissed off, because it was going to be an incredible sell for me, but these things happen quite regularly. I have to laugh when I see videos of me uploaded to porn sites with titles such as 'Watch me ream my hot stepsister' or, in this case, 'Anal massacre'. Whatever pleases the algorithm, I guess.

Doing porn shoots back to back is intense. You've got to be a strong person and you've got to like what you're doing – if you're only doing it for the money, your distaste for it will eventually catch up with you. I'm thankful I got to hang out with and work with some of my all-time heroes.

I look back at these films from just a few years ago, and so much has happened in my life since that it almost feels like I was another person. I look different, too – on those trips to the States I was covered in tattoos, including a full sleeve, and I've since had them lasered off. I got my tatts when I was young and in New Zealand, battling with my anorexia and completely messed up from James. The needle piercing my skin felt therapeutic at the time, and I also liked the idea of transforming into someone else, leaving the old Kayla behind. It was almost a form of self-harm. Starting that journey of getting rid of the tattoos made me feel so much better. It was like a goodbye to that sorry past and another chance for that sad girl.

Entering the Porn Olympics

Ever seen a gymnast clap powder onto their hands while staring into the middle distance? They're completely in the zone, running through their routine.

That's me before filming a scene.

Adult entertainers aren't just entertainers, they're athletes. I used to compete in dancing when I was young – contemporary jazz, hip-hop, that kind of thing – and the training for that was *nothing* compared to what's needed to film a scene.

Female porn actors contort, dilate and squirt using muscles most people don't even know exist. To film a scene with one of the biggest dicks in the industry is an incredible feat of endurance, let alone filming a gangbang. A lot of women in the industry take real pride in being able to withstand the sort of physical brutality most people never could. It's comparable to the ultrarunner or the fighter who keeps on pushing through the pain. Even besides the pummelling of throat, ass and pussy (so much porn is as aggressive as possible these days), there's the sinewy clenching into unnatural positions under hot lights. Even before you start shooting, you have an hour of still photos, contorting yourself into positions for minutes on end. Stomach in, back arched, legs splayed. Periodically you'll do that throughout the shoot, too. Start, stop, click; start, stop, click. There could be ten people on set, with the make-up artist constantly darting in to do touch-ups, or to swipe a girl's ring with a baby wipe, or to mop sweat off a guy. During breaks, performers slug Gatorade or eat bananas for energy. It's insane. Quite possibly you'll also be starving, because you have an anal scene and have sensibly fasted beforehand.

Contrary to popular belief, the male performers don't have it much better. Many of my overconfident clients have let me know that a) they've seen my porn, and b) they could do porn, but the reality is they would have to maintain an erection for ten to twelve hours, then pop on cue. There are concerns about Viagra's long-term impact on the heart, and in the short term a guy might suffer priapism, where he can't lose his erection and it becomes really painful. Without fail my clients shut up about it when I mention the friction burns they'd get when their penis is rubbing up against another man's penis in a girl's butthole.

There are ways to prepare for hours of pounding. Some women ice their cooch using silicone dildo moulds filled with water and put in the freezer, or they use numbing cream like the type you're sometimes offered before getting a tattoo. For anal, many women wear a butt plug right up to the moment of shooting, or stretch and soften themselves with a lubed dildo. There's such a process for anal: fasting, douching or having an enema, sniffing amyl nitrate to loosen up. I never prepare, because I'm a machine. Honestly, I just take it straight. It's better in the long run, because if you numb yourself you won't feel it if you tear or if you're getting some kind of injury.

Then there are the specialty scenes. If you're required to spew during a messy blow job, you'll need to drink pints of milk beforehand. If the director wants you to squirt and you're not a squirter, you'll probably have to drink heaps of water to make yourself pee a bit at the right moment. As you can imagine, the smells on set are pungent. There's cum, lube, baby oil, sweat. You can always tell when someone in catering or hair and make-up is a stand-in for the regular person, because they'll look like they've parachuted into a battlefield. For people not used to it, the animalistic side of porn can be way too real and confronting.

Even before I performed in porn, I'd watched so much of it that my sexual fantasies tended to be from the point of view of a camera – which means I very much have a male gaze. That gets even more weird when I'm being eaten out during a porn shoot and in my mind I'm imagining watching porn. It's like Russian dolls, one reality nested inside another. I've always loved watching porn where the lady is fetishised at the beginning: a faceless voice behind the camera asks her to turn around in a circle, maybe pull down her top and show her boobs, as if she accidentally wandered off the street and into this slick Airbnb but still happens to be completely game for a hoedown. I got to live that dream a few times, like when I recorded with Jules Jordan, a director in his fifties who regularly works with my all-time girl crush Angela White. Jules shoots point-of-view, so you never see him, just the girl – or the girl and whoever else wanders into shot to fuck her. Jules had me walk up and down by the pool of his rented apartment, wearing lingerie and towering heels. He followed my butt up some steps that I climbed extremely carefully, trying not to totter on those spikes.

It was a British performer called Keiran Lee who first invited me out to the States. He'd hit me up on Instagram, asking if I wanted to shoot some scenes for Brazzers, a legendary production company that he did some directing for. My first film for them was with Zac Wild, whose trademark was fucking girls absolutely saturated in baby oil. He took that very seriously. The film started with slow-mo footage of me drizzling baby oil all over myself. I'd had my hair styled and my make-up was immaculate, so I was terrified I was going to end up with ratty extensions. Zac manoeuvred me about like a mannequin through every position, then squirted me with even more oil so that he could piston in and out of my ass.

Before we started filming, Keiran had asked if I could squirt. I can – I can splatter the walls – but I downplayed it, because I was worried my pussy might get camera shy on the day. As it happened, I wound up squirting so hard that my cum hit the cameraman and the producer. They were ecstatic. There's a real trend for porn shoots to be hectic and over the top. Sometimes girls will act the shit out of a scene, rolling their eyes back in their heads or going cross-eyed.

After that shoot, there was oil absolutely everywhere: on the doorhandles, on the taps, on my clothes, on the seat of the cab. When I got back to my hotel room, all I wanted to do was take a long hot bath, the water dotted with pools of oil, lazily rubbing my clit at the memories that I could finally now enjoy in full since I wasn't being recorded from every angle.

Keiran and I also did some independent shoots, where he'd hold the camera in his hand, gonzo-style. In one, he shot me and a girl called Bella Blu on a bed in an Airbnb. Keiran was heavy breathing behind the camera and directing us, but I didn't need direction – I took control. I ripped my own lacy teddy so that my cooch was exposed, and then ripped Bella's lingerie, too. She loved my pierced nipples, so I pushed my titties into her mouth, sighing as she rolled her tongue around the tips. Bella lay back so I could eat her out and I dribbled a long string of spit onto her pussy before getting to work on her clit.

'You're such a good girl,' I told her as she sucked Keiran's cock. We closed the scene with her lying beneath me in a sixty-nine and licking his balls as he fucked me from behind. Applause, applause.

I was happy that Keiran had paired me up with Bella, because I hadn't been able to find many female stars to work with. If they already had big followings, they were unlikely to check their DMs – because of creeps (like me) wanting to fuck them. So I would mainly work with men, which was exhausting. The days and weeks were long; the cocks, longer. I'd get back to my hotel completely beat, flopping down on the sofa and leaving tan ass prints on it. Porn is so messy and no number of wet wipes can fix that. I was filming two or three scenes a day to make sure I got my money's worth out of those long-haul flights. I wanted to push myself to get to the top, not because I'm super-competitive but because I want to make as much money as possible and then bow out.

Not All Porn Is Equal

'Are you okay in there?' The concierge rapped on the door once more. I'd bolted to the toilet in the lobby before he could see me cry.

'I'm fine,' I sobbed brightly. 'I promise I won't be much longer.'

I wildly circled my hair with a spray of dry shampoo, trying to give it some more oomph. I'd already applied my make-up thickly, but every time I had another cry I'd have to touch it up again. I leaned on the basin and took three deep breaths, psyching myself up in the mirror. *Don't cry again.* This made me cry again, and I savagely stabbed at my cheeks with a concealer wand. *For fuck's sake.*

Eventually I made it out of the toilet and asked the concierge to call me a cab, flashing him my best game face: sunny and capable.

The thing about going out on your own on OnlyFans, and then in porn, is you have to do *everything* yourself. If I were shooting with a production company, they'd do hair, make-up and lunch; hook me up with a sexual health service for my checks; provide any paperwork; advise me on visas and travel; maybe even send a car for me. Really, all

I'd have to do before a shoot would be douche, limber up and adopt a good attitude. Going it alone is a whole different ball game.

While in the States I had managed to get a shoot with Johnny Sins, who is the absolute GOAT of contemporary porn. Everyone wants to work with him. Johnny is an industry pro in his mid-forties, with a shaved head and blue eyes. Brazzers cast him more than a thousand times in their films, to the point where there were memes depicting him in his many professions – plumber, doctor, firefighter, teacher, cop. *Vice* even called him 'The hardest-working man in the world.'

But then Johnny realised he could make a better living and have more artistic control if he set himself up on OnlyFans and shot and distributed his own videos. So he and I arranged to do a few shoots together, for which neither of us would get paid but we'd both have a copy of the footage and could sell it to our own subscriber bases. Increasingly this is the way that savvy adult stars are choosing to work: cutting out the production companies and other middle men. Rather than get a flat rate of, say, $2500, which a production company might pay for a short shoot, we'd both get the content to sell. It made so much more sense, particularly when people just bootleg porn from legacy porn companies and upload it onto sites such as Pornhub for free, so no one wins.

I liked what I'd heard about Johnny's hard work ethic and his good nature. He was also married, to a fellow porn star, and they were clearly making that work. I guessed I was allowed to find him attractive – and I did.

Early that morning I'd been due to fly from LA to Las Vegas, where Johnny had a place, which would leave me plenty of time to beautify and eat lunch and get myself in the zone. When I got to LAX, though, a storm had grounded my plane, and there was no sign of any other flights opening up for the foreseeable future. I had a meltdown at the desk, in front of the stony-faced ground crew, who'd seen it all before. A few metres away from me at another desk, another girl was wailing that she just *had* to get to Vegas for her friend's hens' night. I wasn't about to blubber 'But I have to get railed by Johnny Sins this afternoon – he's the GOAT!' so I just wandered out onto the concourse in a daze and booked an Uber. LA wasn't far from Vegas, was it? In my mind, both cities were hot, bedazzled and full of tanned folk. They couldn't be that far apart.

'Are you sure about this?' the cab driver said, after I'd chucked my cases into the boot.

'Please, just do it,' I said, and settled in to fret-scroll on my phone.

So it turns out that Vegas is a four-hour drive from LA, and that's without traffic. What's your most expensive cab trip ever? Was it $4000? No? Then I win. Weeping, I got out of the car and dragged my cases to the front desk.

'Sorry, Ms East,' the receptionist said. 'Your payment has been declined.'

It turned out the cab trip from hell had triggered a warning at my bank back in Australia and my account had been frozen. I stood there like an idiot with a queue building up behind me as I tried to call the number in Australia, but I was too stressed to cope with the multiple-choice options I was been given.

'Give me a minute,' I implored the receptionist, and dragged my cases to the toilet by the lifts to have a simultaneous meltdown and glow-up.

Thankfully, the messages I'd been getting back from Johnny all morning seemed set on putting my mind at rest.

Don't worry, girl – you'll get here when you get here. I'm just chilling.

Johnny was as chill in real life as he was on his socials, which are largely followed by thirsty women. No wonder: he's such a hottie. He immediately made me feel at home. There was no crew waiting impatiently, either: Johnny had set up one camera on a tripod by the bed, with another ready for hand-held point-of-view shots. When we were ready to go, I put on a tiny set of red lingerie and joined him on the bed.

If I could give any future clients a 101 in having sex, it would be in the form of the video I made with Johnny that day. This sex was like a symphony, building from flirtation to fucking to lovemaking and back again.

With the camera rolling, Johnny took my face in both hands and kissed me really deep. You'd never guess that his body count would be in the thousands, because he treated me with wonder, as though he couldn't believe his luck that he got to make out with a beautiful girl. He took his time, too; a million miles away from the aggressive, gymnastic shoots I'd been on lately.

I pulled his shorts down and released his cock. 'Let's see what you're working with,' I purred, as if I hadn't already studied it online like I was cramming for exams. Johnny held eye contact with me as I crawled towards him on the bed. He gently bunched my hair in his hand so I could suck his dick, which was gorgeous-looking. I forced my own throat down onto it until it was laden with spit. It was really turning me on the way Johnny kept sucking in his breath, as if trying not to blow already.

'You're so fucking hot,' he moaned.

I leisurely fucked his cock with my mouth, vibing on the rhythmic suction noise each time it hit the back of my throat. For a good ten minutes I only paused to occasionally gasp for breath.

When I felt Johnny subtly shifting his position, I sat up and released my titties from my bra. He murmured his approval. I'd been getting a good tan while sunbaking in my bikini in LA, so I had the authentic teardrop tan line that I'd ogled in porn clips when I was younger. I smooshed my boobs in Johnny's face.

Johnny pulled me onto his lap to straddle him. He sucked each of my tits in turn, locking eyes with me again. I swear the guy wanted to eat me whole. When he pushed me onto my back and pulled aside my tiny red g-string to bury his face in my pussy, I didn't have to fake it. He sucked on my clit slowly and rhythmically, making me cum for real.

By the time he was ready to penetrate me, I was dying for his cock. Johnny knelt above me and slowly, slowly, slowly pushed into my wet pussy. Holding eye contact, he licked his fingers and gently rubbed my clit. He picked up the pace, then leaned forwards and took my face in his hands again, French-kissing me as he continued to fuck me. He grabbed the point-of-view camera and kept fucking me in missionary. Later, when I watched back, I saw what my clients saw: what it was like to fuck Kayla Jade. The camera had the perfect view of my bouncing tits and the sheer lust on my face.

Johnny used his shoulders to push my legs right back so he could fuck me as deep as possible. Then I was on top, my tits slapping his face. I leaned right back so he had a good view of his cock pistoning in and out of me. When we switched to doggy, he pushed down on my shoulders, allowing him to angle down from above. When he needed to catch his breath we didn't stop. We just lay on our sides so we could slowly smooch and fuck.

'Aww, Jesus,' he moaned when we went back to doggy again, this time with him filming my butt bouncing up and down the length of his cock. Just as I thought things couldn't get any better, he pulled me to the end of the bed on my back and ate my pussy again. I felt no pressure to perform – every moan and squirm was for real.

Then it was his turn. 'Cum for me, baby,' I said. He thrust a few times inside my pussy, then pulled out and shot his load on my perfectly shaved slit. 'Fucccck,' he said, burying his still-spasming cock inside me one more time.

Forty fucking incredible minutes later, we were done.

That shoot with Johnny felt so natural. We could laugh and play, and there was no icky feeling like I got from some shoots: that some young tugger somewhere would be learning how to pressure and push around a girl by watching it. It just proves that porn doesn't need to be frantic to be a turn-on. Seeing genuine lust on screen is way hotter.

If I could hang on to this feeling, I'd be a happy, happy girl, I thought.

The Time I Thought I'd Die

For the most part, my experiences in porn have been positive, with male performers going out of their way to take care of me and give me advice. There was one horrific exception: a collab with a content creator I'll call Xavier.

Have you ever seen those consent clips that sometimes run before a particularly aggressive porn scene? The female performer smilingly explains that she loves rough sex and is really happy to be doing this – so you can go right ahead and jerk off without any guilt whatsoever. News flash: these videos mean nothing. Not when the woman has no idea what she's about to get into, because every single 'hard no' that she's communicated is about to be bulldozed.

It was on one of my solo trips to the States to work with as many established names as possible that I found this out for myself. I've mentioned the financial advantages of cutting out production companies and doing collabs with independent creators, but there is one obvious disadvantage: most of the time it will just be you and the other person in the room, with no one to hold them accountable. This is how Xavier came to prey on so many girls who were new to the industry.

Xavier had gone out of his way to associate with some of the top female names in porn. Newer entertainers like me looked up to these women, so of course we wanted to work with Xavier. He wasn't bad-looking, either: much younger than most male performers, and known for his good-quality videography.

Before we met, Xavier love-bombed me with messages, gushing about how much he dug my content and my Kiwi accent. When I got out of the Uber at his house, he greeted me very warmly. We hung out for a good hour before shooting, making out a little, and it weirdly felt almost like a date. I was actually crushing on this guy. He talked about where he would take me for dinner afterwards and all the sights he could show me around town. I'll admit, I was charmed. Girl, it just shows how much you can change in a couple of years, because Kayla Jade now would 100 per cent see that kind of chat as a red flag. And that's the kind of hard-earned wisdom I hope to pass on to you, too, because it's not just creators who can have their boundaries violated – it's everyone.

I noticed that Xavier talked about himself a lot: about how he progressed so quickly, and how he was the best male performer around. But I just thought he had a big ego, and I was well used to that type.

When we were ready to start filming, Xavier led me into a room where he'd created a cute pastel-coloured set, where he could shoot professional-looking reels of the female talent. The bed was covered in girly pillows and stuffed animals. The effect was to make a woman seem younger, more innocent and submissive. I happily posed coquettishly on the bed, excited about our session together and the rapport we had.

This collab was meant to be normal boy-girl content. I knew it was going to be a little rougher – because that was Xavier's style – and that was okay. I had already made it clear what I would and wouldn't do. At the top of the 'no' list was anal. I hadn't prepped, and I had an upset stomach from all the travelling I'd been doing. So we shot the consent video and we were good to go.

When Xavier pressed record, the energy completely changed. Too late, I realised that I was in big trouble. Again, you don't need to be in a porn situation to experience what I went through. The modus operandi of this kind of guy is to very quickly overwhelm the woman. Get rough fast and not quit, so that she doesn't know which way is up.

The whole time he was manhandling me, Xavier was talking, though I barely registered his words at the time. He told the viewers I'd come all the way over from Australia, and kept calling me Thicc Malibu Barbie. All I was focusing on was the fact that his eyes had changed, like a shutter had come down. They were completely dead.

Xavier wrapped his hands around my throat and dug in his thumbs, squeezing painfully until I almost lost consciousness. Repeatedly, he hit me in the face with his open hand, hard, saying awful derogatory stuff one minute, then the next minute flattering me. He manipulated me into doing vomit content, deliberately forcing his cock so far down my throat that I kept throwing up. All my hard limits, which I'd communicated so carefully, were being breached.

When it came to anal – my hardest no – Xavier kept up a campaign of pressure. He kept moving the goalposts: couldn't he just lick my ass for a moment? Couldn't he just push his cock in real quick, since it was what he was known for? He had some lube right here, see? Xavier took a bottle of baby oil and shoved it into my ass, squeezing the oil inside.

He forcefully backdoored me repeatedly so that the oil would squirt out.

But the worst things happened when he turned off the camera. Periodically, he would stop recording and say, 'Alexa, turn the timer on for thirty seconds.' During the time the camera was off he would say super-degrading things to me and act even worse. He knew I had kids, but he tried to make me role-play that I was his heavily pregnant wife, all while hitting me around the head. When he actually stomped on my head, I completely dissociated.

You can tell in a video if a woman has checked out. Her eyes are vacant. She appears to be in shock. She *is* in shock. She goes through the motions. Mentally, I had completely checked out. Physically, my body shut down. In one of the periods when the timer was on, he was backdooring me hard and I had some leakage because my guts weren't right. In my peripheral vision I saw him wipe it up with his fingers and suck them clean. I couldn't believe what was happening.

I don't know if creating this thirty-second countdown was just to further intimidate me and mess with my head, but I heard from other girls later that he did the same thing with them. Xavier relentlessly kept things moving without offering a break, manipulating me like a doll. I just focused on the fact that it would all be over soon – one way or another.

Around three hours later, we were finally done. And then, just like that, Xavier was back to being a lovey-dovey charming guy, like we'd just had so much fun, like we were in on this together. He talked about a cool Mexican restaurant he wanted to take me to and suggested he call me later after I'd chilled out at my hotel. I have no idea what I said in return, but it would have been something amenable. Xavier ordered me an Uber and, while we waited for it, he showed me his bathroom, where he had lots of anal-care stuff and the morning-after pill, as if he was a really sweet guy who understood the etiquette of BDSM. He was clever. At this point, my body was exhausted. I was just defeated.

~

Around 2017 or 2018, the porn industry finally had its own Me Too moment. A new generation of cam girls held directors, producers and actors in their fifties and sixties accountable for multiple rapes and cases of coercion. Some of these men did jail time. This was good news for sex workers, who were used to not being taken seriously by the police or the judicial system, as if we were another species when it came to reporting sexual assault, with different rules surely to apply.

'The women have come up with a narrative that is unbelievably similar,' protested one such dinosaur on Louis Theroux's *Forbidden America* series, in an episode called Porn's Me Too. Yeah, no shit, dude. He later got nine months.

These days, porn productions have really stringent consent forms, but still, generally speaking, the smaller the production, the bigger the risk. I've heard plenty of horror stories about two-man production companies. So by that logic it's not surprising that content creators – men working with no team at all – can get away with near-murder. Honestly, the collab world is the Wild West. Anyone can be a creator and there is zero regulation because the law hasn't caught up to the evolution of the industry. It means that guys who have a hidden agenda can act upon their sick thoughts by establishing themselves as a creator, and using their skills in marketing and videography as a legitimate front for abusive behaviour and misogyny.

We need more awareness about the kind of playbook used by narcissistic creators such as Xavier. The fact that they get such big viewing numbers makes them seem professional to naive girls, but actually it just means there are a lot of sick guys out there who want to watch other sick guys' fantasies. Xavier was one of the biggest creators on OnlyFans for a reason: because so many guys love watching women be degraded and humiliated. I think the majority of men who watched Xavier's content would *love* the fact that most of it was actually non-consensual.

Content seems to be getting more and more extreme. Men who watch a lot of porn become desensitised to it, so they always have to search for something worse: slapping, waterboarding (seriously), women's heads being pushed into toilets or dog bowls, extreme degradation. The brain quickly adapts to novelty.

My advice to content creators would be to always make sure you check references. Make a safety plan for each time you work with someone, and communicate that with other creators. There is always strength in numbers. For ages I only told my two best friends about my experience with Xavier, because the idea that I had been dumb or naive, or just not able to handle the kind of shit other women did, kept me quiet. Filming the consent video was Xavier's manipulative way of letting me know that if I told anyone about what happened they wouldn't believe me.

Xavier edited the video of our encounter and sent me a copy. I wasn't about to let him make all the profit from my ordeal, so I uploaded it to my OnlyFans, even though I couldn't watch it myself. A lot of my loyal subscribers couldn't watch either and messaged me to say that they didn't want to see me like that; but there was also a large percentage of my following who it turned out really *did* want to see me get roughed up. The sad thing is, to this day it's my best-selling video, and even though I've now deleted it, people search for it. What the fuck has happened to men that they would be so into sexual assault and hurt-core?

I got some criticism for sharing that video. I saw comments on TikTok saying that I made a lot of money out of it so I can't complain. To that, I'd say, let's not blame victims for how they respond to their own sexual assaults. Then there are those comments from people who have the mentality of 'Well, I went through something like that too, so just get over it – *I* had to.' That attitude saddens me so much. It's a defensive response that plays right into predators' hands. It does their dirty work for them, making victims afraid to speak up.

There will always be women in a predator's orbit who will defend him by protesting, 'He didn't do that to *me*.' But predators will show a different version of themselves depending on who they're interacting with. They can be totally cool with people they think have more power than them, or who they can use to get to the top. To not acknowledge that is to do a huge disservice to other women.

There was some good news out of all this. Not long after we filmed, an anonymous X account was made to document everything that girls were saying about Xavier, with the aim of cancelling him. I made some TikTok videos to add my voice to the crowd. There were common themes: the love-bombing, the manipulation, the choking to the point of passing out, the off-camera periods and the super-violent acts, the making us do backdoor. People started sending this evidence to his family members. They messaged all the big platforms he was on, so all his accounts wound up being deleted. Someone even carved 'rapist' into his car.

Xavier's defence was along the lines of: 'You hung out with me after it happened. Here are our nice messages.' When a girl talked about how she'd had her head stomped on, he shared screen shots of the messages from her afterwards, where she was acting normal. Thankfully, people are starting to understand this kind of delayed response to trauma now. It takes a lot of time for someone to process what they are feeling, or to get over the fear they have around that person. Quite often, someone who has been sexually assaulted will actively stay connected with their abuser in an attempt to minimise the trauma in their own mind. So many judges in court cases in decades gone by have expressed disbelief that this happens, not understanding that a victim is desperately trying to normalise her situation and to regain a feeling of control. Eventually, as she starts to process what happened to her – often through hearing other people's stories – she will back away from the perpetrator.

In a way, I'm glad this happened to me early on. It taught me a whole bunch of red flags that all women need to look out for, such as men who love-bomb so that their victim craves the abuser's 'good' behaviour and dismisses the abuse as a weird blip, and all the different forms that coercion can take. These days I've got a sixth sense. My baseline is to always assume a man has some sort of agenda unless he proves otherwise. I'm not impressed by money or celebrity and I can spot a fake, narcissist or misogynist a mile off. As a sex worker, I'm learning everything there is to know about men, way more than the average human will ever need to learn. Lucky them.

So what became of Xavier? Well, he was kicked off all his platforms and he scrubbed away his internet footprint. Last I heard, he was trying to make a comeback via his girlfriend's platform. Since his videos were all point-of-view, people never saw his face, potentially making it easy for him to relaunch under a different name. Although, let's not forget that plenty of men would celebrate him and would very happily watch anything he puts out under his own name. The scary thing is, predators like that will always find sick sycophants to support them.

Everything You Ever Wanted to Know About Full Service

When people imagine my dream client, they picture someone around forty: sophisticated, good-looking, a bit of silver at the temples. We have a dinner date, he orders me the wagyu and a bottle of Cristal. Giggling at all the stares as we leave, we tumble into an Uber, then head back to the hotel for mutually satisfying sex.

That's cute. But no. My dream client was a Spanish salsa teacher, Alonzo, with a bum-fluff moustache, a pouty lower lip that would get stuck to mine when we kissed, and nervous, puppy-dog eyes. He'd hold doors open for me to the point of being annoying, had a small cock and loved anal. That meant it would sometimes end up being a $20,000 booking, for the honour of a sex act that I hardly felt. Because he was so humble, I'd always put on a show of begging him to show me some salsa moves, which would chew up twenty minutes of his booking. He always graciously agreed, though he stopped short of letting me upload them to TikTok. I miss Alonzo. On one particularly sweet booking we had barely there sex, then he fell asleep. I lay there, very still, not moving, as the hours ticked by.

If this sounds like the easiest job in the world, please consider all the bullshit I have to go through with men ceaselessly messaging me, which I *don't* get paid for. There are the explicit messages, where they're just getting off on forcing their way into my inbox; the insulting messages, where they call me names, tear down my appearance and say they wouldn't even fuck me with someone else's cock; and the time-wasting messages, where they want attention but you just *know* they're never going to book. Those last ones make me particularly angry. It's literally like you're talking to someone from Facebook Marketplace. *Hi. Hi. Hi. Is this still available?* So when a new guy messages me I just send one long initial message back with every possible detail in it. If they ask me something else after that, I know they're only there to test my patience.

Welcome to the world of full service. The first question men and women alike are dying to ask when they meet me – whether we're in a hotel room, in a supermarket queue, doing a media interview or at the school gates – is how being a full-service sex worker *works*. As if we're talking about a hadron collider, rather than the oldest profession in the world. The second most common question is 'HOW much?' – accompanied by bulging eyes and a tone of utter disbelief. But I'll get to that one later.

I get it, because I had all these questions, too, when I was starting out on OnlyFans and considering my other options – to go balls deep into seeing clients or not. It took time to befriend other sex workers and find my tribe, before I could start asking the same questions. So let me use this chapter to second-guess all the things you might like to know about sex work.

What should you call me?

I talk about being an 'SW' on TikTok so that I don't get kicked off the platform, but what about 'escort', 'hooker' or 'prostitute'? 'Prostitute' and 'hooker' now carry a lot of stigma, so my advice would be to refer to me as an escort if you're talking to your nan or a sex worker if you're talking to your mates.

Is it legal?

I've had amazing luck in my career, not only by hooking into OnlyFans just as it was taking off, but also with my timing in taking up full-service sex work. In 2019, sex work was decriminalised in the Northern Territory, followed by Victoria in 2022 and Queensland in 2024. The Australian Capital Territory and New South Wales were well ahead of the rest of the country, decriminalising most sex work in 1992 and 1995 respectively. Did the ACT go first because it has the most politicians in residence? We can't be sure. We do know that before sex work was decriminalised in these places, sex workers might have had trouble opening a bank account and landlords might have refused to take a sex worker as a tenant.

Sex work still isn't fully legalised in Tasmania, where you can be self-employed but not work in a brothel or on the streets. In Western Australia, a sex worker can work from a hotel or their own home. But as Scarlet Alliance, the national sex workers association (and your go-to for any legal questions), points out, 'local councils, landlords and building management organisations (strata or body corporate) may prohibit sex work in residential areas. This places independent/private sex workers at risk of eviction.' South Australia is the strictest of all. The law there considers a hotel to be a brothel if a sex worker is operating within it.

If I go there on tour, hotel staff could report me if they get suss. I just don't rub it in their faces.

How do I find my clients?

In the early days, it was hard. Advertising sex work on OnlyFans is a big no-no – you'll get banned. When subscribers first got wind that I was doing full-service work, they would constantly message me on OnlyFans about it and I'd have to block them straight away.

For me, it's been word-of-mouth. Other sex workers on the Gold Coast might have clients who want to 'shop around' – quite often, a guy will consider himself a collector, determined to sample the whole range of sex workers who have a social media presence, as if he's collecting watches or cigars. There's an implicit understanding that if another girl is generous with her contacts, you should be generous right back and recommend clients of your own.

I never paid my dues in a brothel – fuck that. I had sex worker friends who told me how unsafe brothels could be. A booking might only cost a guy $300, and not require him to show ID. This doesn't filter out the bad players, and I've heard of girls getting raped and stalked home. Also, the people who own brothels take a massive cut of a girl's earnings. I'm glad I didn't start full service until I was twenty-nine, because if I was fresh at eighteen I probably would have got myself into some terrible situations.

I've always been independent, setting up profiles on websites that are escort-owned and -operated, uploading pictures, my info and my rates. It's a full process signing up to these websites. To get verification you have to write your name, the date and the site name on a piece of paper and take a photo of yourself holding it. Sometimes you have to do it naked; I don't know why. But you need to be verified so that someone doesn't try to pass themselves off as you. That's a scam to get men to leave deposits, at which point Fake Kayla vamooses with their money. I've had random men message me and say, 'How dare you ghost me?' They've been scammed out of thousands of dollars because they thought that they were messaging me, but they were actually chatting with some dude who had taken my Instagram photos and set up a fake profile. One guy told me he'd got into credit card debt because of it. I felt a bit sorry for him, but I wasn't about to become his penpal. He should have looked into it more carefully. People steal my identity all the time. Some random escort websites advertise me though I haven't even signed up, just because they want the clout. When Fake Kayla on their sites doesn't answer, the hope is that visitors will look at the other, real profiles.

Who ARE my clients?

People are dying to know what my clients are like, probably imagining them to be bikers, married men, weird degenerates and smelly loners. The truth is, it's a whole cross-section of the population. Picture yourself walking down a city street. It's that student. It's that businessman. It's that guy in gym wear. It's that tradie. It's that couple. They're all just normal people. That's the freaky thing – you never know what kind of secret lives people are living. Of course, I see people in power, too – cops, judges, CEOs, politicians. For them, seeing a sex worker is safer than getting on the apps.

How much prep goes into getting booking-ready?

Before my first client of the day I'll have a shower, shave, moisturise, tan and do my hair and make-up. If I have more than one client – like if I'm on tour interstate – I'll repeat that process between each one to cleanse myself of the bio-soup. Sometimes I'll end up having seven showers in a day, so my tan starts to get really patchy. When I'm not working I rarely wear make-up because my sensory sensitivity means I hate the feeling of thick products clogging my skin. But if I'm on tour I have to constantly reapply it, especially on friction areas such as around the mouth. If a guy wants to cum on my face it will cost extra, because that requires a full goddamn make-up reapplication. Stubble rash is another drama. I prefer it when a guy has a beard, tbh.

How do I choose a hotel?

Unless I'm given specific instructions, I book a reasonably priced suite and pay for it, adding the amount to the figure I quote the client. My regular hotel on the Gold Coast has two-bedroom serviced apartments, overlooking the water. There's a supermarket downstairs so I can nip down for anything I've forgotten, such as mouthwash or make-up wipes, and there's a spa and sauna if the client can be persuaded to waste an hour of his booking just chilling out.

If I'm on tour, like in Sydney, I'll get a serviced apartment, because it will have a kitchen and a washing machine. Towels are always a problem when you're seeing back-to-back clients, because you run out, and the hotel doesn't care if the two they gave you are coated with DNA. So being able to wash them helps. That and calling down to reception the moment I get there, to sweetly let them know that housekeeping must have forgotten to leave me any towels. When I've got a couple of clients booked for one day, having a two-room apartment means they both get a freshly made bed to fool around on – only polite, right?

Sometimes the client wants to book a flash hotel. If that's the case, I'll arrange to get there early so I can have fun filming content for TikTok: giving people a tour, raiding the minibar. I also like to acclimatise to the space and relax into it, so that when the client arrives they're more nervous than I am. After they've gone, I'm out of there. You might think it would be nice to sleep in a fancy hotel, but actually no – not when the sheets are covered in XY chromosome gunk and it smells of sex. It's a bit like watching porn: the minute you've climaxed, you slap down the laptop screen in disgust at what you've just seen. Also, that hotel is my work environment. Would you want to sleep in your workplace?

Very occasionally I'll visit a client at his home, but only if I know him really well or he's got a really good write-up from sex workers I trust. Home visits are where all the bad stuff happens ... even if it's just that you have to fuck on some stained mattress in a student share house with people gaming loudly in the lounge room.

What do I pack?

If it's an overnight stay I have a little suitcase on wheels, but otherwise I use my Christian Dior tote. Inside there's a little money bag, make-up, refresher wipes, disposable toothbrushes, mouthwash, and condoms in multiple sizes – because I could be seeing someone who has a micro pee-pee. I have to buy special 'snug' condoms online because I've learned from my mistake of trying to put a normal condom on someone with a micro penis: it just hangs loose. One guy with a micro penis just wanted me to lick his nipples for the whole session. By the end of it, my tongue was as dry as the Sahara Desert. It was a real endurance test.

I'll pack my favourite vibrators that are guaranteed to make me squirt, and my dildo that looks freaky disappearing inside me. Guys are legit fascinated by that stuff. If it's an overnighter I'll also pack snacks and a douche, in case he wants to do anal. I don't like being surprised with a request for anal, but then, it does drive up the overnight price from $12,000 to $15,000, so there's that.

What happens when the client arrives?

Before we meet we'll have already discussed what the client requires, my dos and don'ts, and that he should have the money ready upfront if he hasn't already transferred it to my bank account. I always meet the client in the lobby so that I can be sure the receptionists will see him – there's nothing illegal about what I'm doing, and them getting eyes on the guy feels like an extra layer of safety. I *want* the staff to be gossiping about us the moment we're out of earshot. I always get a thrill of excitement, stepping out of the lift into the lobby. There have been a couple of occasions where I've got the idea that a guy will look a certain way and then it's someone completely different, and I think, holy shit, I was not expecting *that*. Once, I was waiting outside reception to meet a client called Joe and he was messaging me, telling me he was there, but the only person I could see was an old woman on her phone. I sidled up to her, thinking maybe it was a 'Jo', not a 'Joe'. Thank god the real Joe walked up just before I got trashy.

As soon as I shake the guy's hand – or give him a hug, whichever he wants to do in front of the hotel staff – I'm assessing the shit out of him. What's his energy? If someone's off, I can tell in the first five seconds. Up in the room, I'll count the money in front of him and then he'll go have a shower. I will already have arranged soap, mouthwash, a toothbrush and toothpaste for him to use, because hygiene is king. In the main bedroom I'll have music playing and candles lit. Condoms of all sizes will be right next to the bed, along with some lube.

If I think I can get away with it, I'll get into some small talk to cut into our time. I'm so used to this kind of chat that I don't care if it feels awkward. A game of 'Let me guess the suburb' is a great time-waster if he's local.

By the end of the day I could be holding a lot of cash, particularly if I'm on tour seeing back-to-back clients. I'll keep it in the hotel safe because I've heard horror stories of clients jumping women and making them hand over their money. When I get a moment I'll take it to an ATM that allows cash deposits.

What does booking a tour involve?

If one client wants me to fly interstate, I'll turn it into a tour and will message previous clients to let them know I'm in their city. I'll hole up in a two-bedroom suite for four or five days and see clients back to back. I'm prepared to take shorter bookings – one to two hours – but I'll cancel the whole trip if I'm going to make anything less than $15,000. I might be seeing up to seven clients a day, so I barely leave the hotel. The way my ADHD brain works, I'm either in full hustle mode or I'm not, so I don't want to fuck around eating out or shopping; I just commit to it being a really full-on four days, and then I'll come home and decompress with the fam. I can make good coin but the losses take an emotional form: I'm exhausted, isolated and jaded by the time I make it back home. At least it means I've bought a big chunk of time to hang out with my kids afterwards.

Don't clients mind that I discuss them in TikTok videos?

The possibility of being roasted on TikTok or my podcast definitely deters some men from seeing me, but the way I look at it, it encourages them to act better. I mean, if you haven't done anything weird or douche-y, what tea is there for me to spill? I've had some clients say, 'Please don't post about me' and I've respected that, but you can bet your ass that any sex worker is messaging her besties the moment you leave the room, to debrief. And it's not like the clients don't talk about *us*, either – there are numerous websites dedicated to men rating sex workers. I avoid looking at them because it's so gross. Guys will complain about dumb shit, or they'll post some overblown fantasy about us having had mind-blowing sex and some incredible connection. I'm not sure which is worse.

How much do I charge?

While I wouldn't walk into a bakery and ask the owner how they've been doing this financial year, I do understand the intrigue about how much a sex worker can rake in. My hourly rate is $2000, but I usually see clients for a minimum of a two-hour booking, making it $4000. That covers the bare minimum: blowjob, a few positions, nothing too extreme. Then they can either cum in a condom or on my body. Anal is extra. Rimming is extra. Overnight is $12,000, but that includes six hours' sleep, which I'm very clear about. The guy can have as much sex as he wants outside of those six hours, but he's not allowed to touch me at all during sleeptime. No spooning. Overnighters are usually with guys who want more of a girlfriend experience, anyway, so it's quite realistic that the girlfriend gets some rest.

What do I do with all my money?

I mainly get paid in cash, because guys don't want sex work itemised on their bank statement – not necessarily because they're cheating, but in case they want to get some kind of loan. Even so, I declare everything. I file my tax returns quarterly through an accountant who has many sex worker clients and understands that our business model has a few streams, such as OnlyFans, porn shoots and other bookings. Because I'm disorganised, I pay extra for my guy to go through my bank account and figure it all out for himself.

A good bean-counter is worth paying more for. Mine has been amazing. Right from the start he said, 'You need to stop being a dumb cunt and sort your shit out.' I believe those were his exact words. And I really needed to hear that, because I spent money as fast as I earned it, on clothes, surgery, make-up and extravagant gifts for the kids. He told me, 'I've had so many athlete clients that made a lot of money and now they've got nothing to show for it. I don't want to see that happen to you.' He's a father figure in that way. Because of him I've now got my three-storey house and I'm well on my way to buying a house for both of my kids. No matter what your job is, always find a good accountant and always file your tax return. That's it. That's the only advice I'm giving you.

The Brothers

It's not unusual for two guys to high-five over my head, but until now I'd never known them to be related.

Caleb had sent his first message a whole year earlier, asking if I would be interested in seeing him next time I was in Sydney. There was a fair bit of time-wasting. I'm used to that. Guys get a kick out of messaging you, detailing what they'd like to do to you, and that satisfies them for a bit. Then they reappear and suggest something else – no doubt tapping away at their phone in the toilet of a family gathering or at their girlfriend's house. Sometimes they'll send you a dick pic or a shot of them shirtless. They get blocked pretty soon if they don't put down a deposit: I've got a three-strikes-and-you're-out rule.

What saved Caleb's neck from the chopping block was that on his third message he revealed that he wanted me to fuck both him and his brother, Cody.

Hi Kayla, just wondering when your next availability was and how much it would cost for me and my brother to book you.

Almost before I'd even finished reading it I was tapping out a message to Eden: 'WTF! Does he mean separately or together?' She sent back bomb and sweat emojis.

Is this a common thing for brothers to do? If so, why was I only learning about it now? If Caleb was older, did that mean he got to go first? Was it a weird power trip on his little bro? A bonding thing, maybe? Because nothing says 'quality time' like spit-roasting a complete stranger.

I decided to reply 'Together or separate?', thinking he'd either be offended – *Separate!* – or would just disappear into thin air.

Almost immediately, Caleb messaged back:

Together, lol. We are coming to the Gold Coast next week if that suits? How much upfront?

Oh wow, so he wasn't going to chicken out. I opened Instagram and looked at his profile. Mid-twenties, dark hair, blue eyes, muscular. Hot, but like, *douche*-hot. There were some pics of him in jiu-jitsu gear, which probably meant he thought he was a dom. There are so many young guys who have watched way too much violent porn and who follow all the manosphere podcasters down the Brazilian jiu-jitsu path, and somehow those two things mesh to become their sole identity: a bro who wants to dominate. They're so predictable – I'd be prepared to bet my hard-earned wealth that these guys did ice baths on the reg. I remember one bodybuilder insisted on sniffing smelling salts before he fucked me and kept trying to wave the little bottle under my nose for a joke. It's always these types who call themselves doms, without having bothered to understand any of the etiquette that comes with proper BDSM play.

Scrolling down, I spotted a post of Caleb shirtless in Bali, clinking beers with another guy who looked suspiciously like him. Okay. So maybe this was Cody. Not bad, not bad. Not as douche-hot as his brother, but not bad. I do like a little stalk of my clients before we meet; it's like window-shopping. It's when a client has no internet presence at all that you've got to worry. In this day and age, it's a red flag that their behaviour is so reliably bad that they don't want to be tracked down.

~

The minute these bros walked through the revolving door of the lobby, I could see they meant business. I caught the women on reception glancing at them as they walked confidently towards me, taking turns to shake my hand like they were there to settle on a property, not rent me by the hour.

Caleb leaned in for a cheek kiss, quickly asserting himself as the brother with the moves. His neck smelled good. They were both clean shaven, hair slicked back, nice belts, nice watches – smartly dressed in a way that was understatedly expensive. They looked a world apart from the usual guys on the Gold Coast, who wore fake tan, fake Versace and loafers. In the lift, as we grinned at each other, they were charismatic and polite. It was surface-level shit but, fuck it, I had to admit I was really attracted to both of them.

When the lift doors opened, I walked out first, so that they had a good view of my ass. I was wearing a tight-fitting pencil skirt and a black blouse with ruffles. That's another good reason to stalk a guy's social media: you can gauge what kind of outfit he'd probably want to see you in.

Usually, when the hotel room door closes behind me, I'm thinking of ways to slow down the action, particularly if it's a two-hour session. Of course there's the non-negotiable showering, but maybe I'll also offer them a shoulder massage, or make small talk, or fix them a drink if there's a fully stocked mini bar. This time, though, I wanted to get straight into it the moment they handed over the cash – partly because I was turned on, but partly because I was a little nervous at being in this new sibling supremacy situation. Sometimes it's easier to jump straight in, because once you've got skin on skin it's cool – you're all friends. Conversation can wait till the first natural break.

As Caleb kissed me, Cody stripped off and stroked his cock. I could tell this was going to be an athletic session, because neither of them were hanging back and they were both on their feet. *They've done this before*, I realised. When Caleb pulled back to breathe, lil brother flipped me on my back and started eating me out. If this was one-upmanship, I didn't hate it. Caleb moved around to my head and lowered his cock into my mouth, his balls bumping my chin. I gagged theatrically on his dick, making plenty of drool.

I really like to look a guy in the eye when I'm sucking his cock, though, so I switched positions and knelt on the bed, guiding Caleb towards me by the dick. I reached for Cody's cock with my free hand, but he pulled away. Okay, so they definitely didn't want any risk of them touching each other. Noted.

'Why don't you fuck me?' I said to Cody. I got onto all fours while continuing to deep-throat his brother. These guys *really* had beautiful cocks. Good genes.

Cody got on the bed and manoeuvred his way behind me, pulling on a condom. I moaned as he pushed his length inside me. Cody started to fuck me long and hard, and after a few dozen strokes was slapping my ass with relish. Was that a twitch of irritation I saw in his brother's face? In any case, my eyes were soon watering as Caleb started fucking my mouth as hard as Cody was railing my pussy. This was anthropologically fascinating: they both wanted to dom me – which is fine by me, I love playing sub – but there's only ever room for one alpha in a room.

We moved through doggy, missionary, cowgirl, back to doggy, and I lost track of who was doing what, but I did notice they never did the tag-team thing of taking turns in the same hole. It was like that was a bridge too far. At no point did they make eye contact with each other, either. I was so confused about why we were all here together.

As we approached the two-hour cut-off, the negative energy I'd been picking up on during the clam jam absolutely exploded. Cody had gone to make himself a whisky on the rocks, and he brought back one for me, but not for Caleb.

'You right, mate?' Caleb snapped, squaring up. His erect cock seemed to add punctuation. I excused myself to take a shower, but I could hear them raging the moment I turned off the water. It sounded like furniture was about to get smashed. Being cautious, I always take my phone into the bathroom with me. I picked it up, ready to call my security guy, who was waiting downstairs. I don't usually have one with me, but if there are multiple male clients, or a job that feels a bit suss, I'll hire one for the night. (He probably did jiu-jitsu, too.)

I heard the door slam shut, so I ventured out. Cody was sat on the edge of the bed, alone, in a towel. 'Sorry about that, hey?' he said. 'He's been a dick all day.'

I was slightly bummed, since Caleb was the brother I was more attracted to, but Cody wound up extending by an hour, which was good because I doubted he had any energy left. Sure enough, we wound up just hanging out by the hotel pool, having another drink. He revealed they'd had some kind of argument earlier and that they'd still been beefing in the Uber over to the hotel. I found that funny. I don't usually cum during a booking, but this time I'd gone all the way to Paris and back. I saw the Eiffel Tower, even as they were having some biblical feud over my back.

On the way home in the car I tried to imagine the arguments:

You always ruin everything.

This is just like the time you wrecked my bike.

Why don't you go running to Mummy?

My phone lit up my face in the dark as I started typing out my debrief to Eden.

~

A few days later I decided do the polite thing and follow up with a message to Caleb, since he was the one who'd organised everything. He'd left without saying goodbye, and I was fully expecting him to start with an apology. Instead, he messaged back and asked me if I wanted to go out with him before he left town, but I decided against it. Money's money, but I actually got off on the Greek play that was the two of them, and I didn't want to ruin the memories.

Caleb and Cody had all the hallmarks of private-school boys. Sharing a girl was like an adult version of soggy biscuit: the game in which fucked-up, horny private schoolboys take turns ejaculating onto a biscuit, with the last one to cum having to eat the whole thing – a twisted rite of passage. Man-boys like Caleb don't worry about how they come across to girls and they certainly don't ever think they need to apologise. These conventionally handsome guys with their privileged perfect cocks just run through women like they're kicking goals, and it's all about who's winning. They fitted the demographic of my clients who went to $60,000-a-year schools and who don't see women as equal, since they know it's the boys who always inherit Daddy's company. Not long after I saw Caleb and Cody, a news story ran about private-school boys in Melbourne who were ranking all their female classmates in a spreadsheet, labelling them as 'wifeys', 'cuties', 'mid', 'object', 'get out' and 'unrapable'. Cool.

After that booking, I made a TikTok video of me counting the money in the hotel robe I'd taken home with me: $3500 cash, $500 deposit, $1500 for the extended time where we hung out by the pool: $5500 in total. Enough to buy me my own silver spoon.

Mummy Issues

Darren was a middle-aged white man with a receding hairline, a bit overweight … you wouldn't pick him out of a line-up, put it like that. The only thing that really stood out about him was his intense loser energy. I know that sounds really mean, but I just can't think of a nicer way to put it.

We were both seated, with me riding his cock, my butt slapping down on his thighs, legs wrapped around him, when I heard him call me 'Mummy'. To be really clear, he didn't call me 'Mama' – it was definitely 'Mummy'. I froze, mid-bounce.

'Yeah, that's it, fuck me, Mummy.'

Dude, I thought. My kids call me that. To paraphrase Will Smith, keep my baby mama name out of your fucking mouth.

Darren's head was mushed into my boobs. I could feel the wetness of his lips sticking to my decolletage. I realised that, the way I was sitting astride him, it was almost like I was holding him, like he was suckling on me. I wanted to spew.

Thankfully, my face was angled over his shoulder so he couldn't see me grimace. I find that it really helps me psychologically if I can be free to make whatever face I feel like during a booking. I'm the master at finding positions and angles to allow myself to go the full WTF.

When Darren left, I showered for ages, scrubbing away at my boobs with the hotel shampoo. I guess Darren had a weird relationship with his mother growing up.

How many times do you hear guys disparagingly saying that a girl has daddy issues? It's meant to mean she's clingy, she's needy, she talks like a baby. But she's got nothing on a guy with mummy issues. Mummy's boys are obnoxious and bratty, like they're stuck at the teenage stage. What's it called? Arrested development. My guess is they've never been told off or pulled into line by their mothers; instead they're treated like little kings. The mother always gets the blame, though, doesn't she? The poor mothers of serial killers are always remembered in history as if they're the ones who did the dismembering.

The problem is, eventually the real world gets to these guys, and they realise that not everybody holds them in such high regard, which causes a schism in their self-worth. These are the men who always message me to whine about something, automatically expecting me to answer. They don't respect any boundaries. They've never heard the word 'no'.

What's really hectic is if these guys end up being successful and earning good money, like they go into finance or some executive kind of job. Because then you have an immature asshole who's on a power trip, overcompensating for that underlying feeling of being completely inadequate, with all the rage that accompanies it. Trust me: that is not a man you want to be hanging out with unless you're getting paid extremely well. In fact, you should leave it to me to take one for the team.

~

Have you seen the 2000 film *Dude, Where's My Car?* There's a 'Super Hot Giant Alien', played by former beauty queen Jodi Ann Paterson, who terrorises Ashton Kutcher and Seann William Scott. By terrorising, I mean she gives them lots of looks up-skirt at her white undies. Her feet come crashing down heavily as she pursues them. She balls her hands into fists and growls.

I swear that movie inspired a giantess fetish in so many millennials; and *Attack of the 50 Foot Woman* would have done the same for boomers. My theory is that guys who are into giant women were once those little boys who rolled around on the floor trying to peek up their mother's dress, earning them a lifelong, rock-hard fetish. My OnlyFans subscribers often get me to shoot custom videos where I'm looking down at them. I step around the camera in high heels, or loom over the lens with my boobs like I'm crushing them. (I've got to be careful, though, as OnlyFans rules are weird about you pretending to smother someone to death with your rack.) Sometimes they want to be shrunk and eaten, too, which is really fiddly to do with the camera. The Japanese call this desire to be consumed vorarephilia, or vore for short. One customer sent me little toy figures to help set the scene and a doll's house that I filmed myself looking through the windows of. Then I came at the camera with my finger and thumb and plucked the imaginary tiny guy up, bringing him up to my mouth until everything went black.

Annndddd: scene.

Honestly, I love the creativity.

There's also the 'muscle mummy' fetish, where men are obsessed with strong girls and will pay insane money to wrestle with them or have their necks squeezed by the woman's thighs in a jiu-jitsu move. Eden's jacked enough to do some of that, being a gym girly, but I just get the one regular guy who wants me to oil up my body in a bikini and flex at the camera. That's all I have to do.

~

For almost a year I was onto a really sweet deal with a guy who wanted to do video calls. Every few nights we'd have a sexy chat. But inevitably, his requests started getting weirder and more mummy-oriented.

Neil was pretty young, maybe twenty-five. In fact, he may even have been living in his mum's house, because his bedroom had that hasn't-moved-out-yet vibe. I could see collectible toys in the background and clothes and plates all over the floor. If his mum didn't come in and scoop all that shit up on the reg and do his laundry, I'd be pretty amazed. Also, the amount of money he was clocking up on these calls – like, $500 a time – there's no way he could have been paying rent. I bet his parents were letting him live there so he could save his money.

Neil would sit in front of his laptop, nude but for his glasses and socks. He'd often be pulling himself off, getting me to describe my day or my last booking. I started getting the vibe that he might enjoy anal play on himself. And, look, I can't tell you definitively how I know these things; I just *know*. As the months ticked on, I'd get him to start fucking his ass with dildos. He warmed to this mission so fast, it was like he'd been waiting his whole life for someone to suggest it. Each time we had a session he'd bought a new, bigger dildo – realistic veined black ones. Ones that came with a remote control and an app, so that I could take charge of them. Ones with names like Anal Annihilator. Ones shaped like an arm and a fist. I'd offer encouragement or give him instructions from my phone, often while feeding the cats with one hand or painting my toenails. Neil was so engrossed in the whole process of lubing and stretching that he'd never notice.

'How do you fucking like that?' he'd say, over and over, maybe to himself – it was hard to tell.

Then Neil started to get into cock and ball torture, which he'd carry out himself. He sent off for a bunch of toys such as a Kali's Teeth bracelet, which snaps around the penis. Spikes attached to the inner rim dig into the penis if it becomes aroused … so it would be my job to tell him he'd been a disgusting little boy to get him hard. The final time we met he'd bought a male chastity device called the Gates of Hell, which completely binds the cock in metal cock rings, bending it painfully so that getting turned on is agony.

And then Neil just disappeared. I guess there's really nowhere to go from there.

I Don't Want to Fuck Your Husband

The guy was having a *really* long shower. I considered leaving, but it would be my responsibility if he trashed the hotel room. Not that he seemed like the type: sleepy eyes, a sexy smile that he flashed every time he made me laugh, laidback, good at eating pussy. He gave off pretty good vibes. But I never rely on vibes.

Finally, he emerged in a cloud of steam, towelling his long hair and shooting me that smile again. He pulled on his jeans and then his socks. I guessed he was deliberately leaving his shirt till last so that I could drink in his ample chest and biceps a while longer. Steroids? Definitely, but with a touch as subtle as a Cordon Bleu chef.

'What are you getting up to this weekend?' I asked, as he finally, reluctantly, pulled his shirt over his head, slowing down its trajectory just above his abs. He sat on the edge of the bed to lever his foot into his boot and looked up at me through his curtain of hair. A practised move.

'It's my bucks' night,' he said. 'We're going to the casino and then on to ... wherever.'

He said it so casually that it took a moment to land.

'Sorry ... *your* bucks' night?'

'*My* bucks' night,' he said, a harder edge creeping into his voice. Suddenly I was just the whore and I should know my place. Certainly, I should be cool with this guy shooting his load mere hours before he walked down the aisle.

These are the moments when I seriously consider jacking in this job. I've often talked about how bookings are just business transactions, but most business transactions don't make you want to hurl the nearest dildo at someone's head. So the next time someone tried to book me and I found out he was about to get married? I blasted him, first name only, in a video, and somehow the TikTok karmasphere did its magic. Days later, his fiancée called off the wedding. Onwards and upwards, girlfriend.

I'm all about monogamy, which is why I'm not currently in a relationship. My little family means so much to me and I can't imagine ever doing anything to jeopardise that in the way so many clients are willing to. Jackson and I are free to date other people, but so far neither of us has – but if we did, we would tell each other. They're our rules, our mutual understanding. Each couple has their own. But when you marry someone, you're telling them they are exclusive to you, unless you both agree otherwise – and I could tell from the way this guy was reacting that he had *not* had that conversation with his betrothed.

'That is shitty, dude,' I said, turning my back on him to pack my case. Actually, it was already packed, but I couldn't stand to look at him, so I just unzipped and zipped it again in a violent motion.

'Oh yeah?'

'Yeah,' I said, wheeling around. 'What the fuck is wrong with you? You should be excited and honoured to be marrying the girl you love.'

His brow darkened and he got up. 'All right, bitch, see you.'

'You're a piece of shit,' I yelled at his back, wishing I had a dildo to hand. The moment the door banged behind him, I blocked his number.

I'm not trying to be a hero by telling you this story, but I do wish that women wouldn't blast sex workers online as though we're literally trying to steal their men, like we tiptoe up behind a guy wearing a wedding ring, whispering, 'Wanna fuck? Wanna fuck?' Listen, I think your cheating husband is gross, and if I get wind that a man is taken before he books me, there's no way I go through with it. Trust me: when you've heard a guy complain, even as he's undressing, that his pregnant girlfriend won't sleep with him anymore, you want to board up your vagina and hang out the 'condemned building' sign. I kicked that guy out, too.

And that's exactly why I'm with most people in finding Bonnie Blue's antics so vile. If you've somehow missed the newspaper stories and documentaries made about her, Bonnie was OnlyFans' most infamous creator, before she got booted off the platform for violating the rules about 'extreme challenges'. People love to hate her, and that's exactly what she capitalises on – she's super-savvy. She's coming for your husbands, she's coming for your sons ... basically, if you've got a man in your life, she can take them away from you and it's your fault.

While people like to heap disgust on Bonnie's porn stunts, such as being fucked by 1057 men in twenty-four hours, it's her soundbites that really get to people. Bonnie claims that cheating partners seek her out because they're not getting satisfied at home and yet are expected to pick up after themselves, which is unfair on men. She told the Australian radio show *Kyle & Jackie O* that being unfaithful makes a guy a better partner, likening it to a reset button: 'Because then you can come home, deal with your wife's whingeing and get on with looking after the kids.' And when one woman claimed on TikTok that she'd found out that her long-term fiancé was one of those 1057 guys, Bonnie commented: 'He only needed somewhere to c~m and p~ss into, he's all yours for cuddles.'

It's just rage-bait content, sure, but the problem for sex workers like me is it reinforces the stereotype that we are insatiable and want to profit off 'normal' women's pain by stealing their men. It's guilt by association.

Bonnie had her visa revoked by the Australian Government in 2024 because she'd put out a call for 'barely legal' men to fuck her at schoolies week; she also did this for spring break in the US and freshers week in the UK, showing a particular interest in virgins. I know it's people's first instinct to laugh that every young boy wishes he could be so lucky, but that's twisted. These are school-aged babies whose brains are still developing. They might sign a consent form, but they don't understand the ramifications of this footage being on the internet forever. And Bonnie's success has spawned a legion of copycat OnlyFans creators who continue to target schoolies.

I'm glad that Bonnie's visa was cancelled, but even headlines about that have an impact on sex workers. I'm already nervous about flying overseas, because sex work isn't legal in every country. A client once flew me to China, which was an adventure, but I'd never risk it now because there's a very public connotation that a woman being on OnlyFans is involved in illegal activity.

~

While I'm clearly no fan of Bonnie, I do want to play devil's advocate for a moment, to look at the hypocrisy that exists around women shooting porn.

It might surprise you to learn that every stunt that Bonnie has drawn hate for is something that men in the porn industry invented decades ago – but they didn't attract the same flack. Let's break this down (and here's a warning: you might want to skip this bit if you're squeamish):

- **Barely legal call-outs:** Don't get me wrong, this idea is sick because it entertains the idea that you should want to fuck someone who *isn't* yet legal. However, 'barely legal' has long been a common genre, both in hetero and gay porn. Larry Flynt – founder of *Hustler* – brought out *Barely Legal* magazine in 1993, of course focusing on young girls. The magazine spawned a whole bunch of copycats and it still exists, including as a video line where 'every episode promises a heart-racing experience of passion just on the edge of maturity'.

- **Targeting schoolies week:** The Girls Gone Wild adult entertainment franchise regularly targeted spring break locations in the US. Filmmakers persuaded intoxicated girls to show their breasts, make out with each other and fuck each other with dildos. In 2005, the founder pleaded guilty to exploitation and for not recording participants' ages.

- **Bodily fluid stunts:** In 2025, Bonnie put a call-out for guys to mail their cum to a PO box, so that she could fill a bathtub and bathe in their rancid man waste. Gross, sure, but John Thompson Productions has been making extreme bukkake (cum on face) and piss videos under its German Goo Girls umbrella since 1997, and there's a huge demand for those kinds of scenes.

- **Record-breaking gangbangs:** In the mid-nineties, director John T Bone arranged for Annabel Chong to have sex with 251 men. The film was released by production company Metro and expanded to a series, with other porn stars and bigger numbers. Some people involved have since admitted that the actual cock counts were way lower than advertised – more like seventy (still a decent effort). The next movie in the series, starring Jasmin St Claire, was advertised as featuring 300 men, but actually there were only thirty on set. In her memoir, *What the Hell Was I Thinking?!!,* Jasmin called that event 'among the biggest cons ever pulled off in the porn business' – but those same kinds of cons still happen today in OnlyFans land.

The only difference between then and now is that Bonnie is cutting out the middle man and pocketing all the money herself. There's a real double standard here. To satisfy men's desires, women in porn have forever been guzzling gallons of cum, getting urinated on and choking on cocks. The moment a woman enthusiastically comes up with her own idea, the mainstream media shows an interest. As long as Bonnie Blue's words generate clicks and views she'll keep cooing about babyface boys and husbands who aren't getting enough, and we'll keep taking the bait.

On paper, Bonnie and I are similar in many ways. Sex workers tend to have led a life on double speed, which can be said for both of us. Like me, Bonnie moved from overseas to the Gold Coast and was married super young to a husband who supported her journey on OnlyFans and worked behind the scenes. We probably share a sense of restlessness and a tendency towards impulsivity, as well as an obvious desire to be at the top of our field. But very unlike me, Bonnie has no fear of judgement. While she's intent on hitting a nerve, I try to be a role model of sorts. I make it clear that there's a personal cost to being a sex worker and I use my experiences to talk about women's safety in general. Almost all my TikTok followers are women, and they come to me because I provide a safe way to explore their fantasies and satisfy their curiosity. I'd never want any woman to feel like I wouldn't have her back.

A Boy Named Peggy

Did I personally imply that Peter Dutton, the leader of the opposition, was Peggy Sue? Absolutely not. Did I inadvertently win Labor the 2025 election in Australia? Maybe.

I lost track of how many TikTok videos I made about one particular client, who I called Peggy Sue: a guy who enjoyed being 'pegged' with a strap-on. I alluded to him being very high profile in his field, in a high-stress job, right at the upper echelons. This was a red rag to a bull: my followers started trying to guess who this guy might be. Then Gold Coast commentator Holly MacAlpine, who mainly addresses politics, suggested that Peggy Sue was Peter Dutton – and the rumour just exploded. I'd never even heard of Holly, but she made multiple videos that generated many headlines and got the comment sections raging.

At first, the real Peggy Sue panicked at all the guessing games, since internet sleuths can be really hardcore ... although, as he said, he was 'both panicking and rock hard'. Then he started to enjoy the roasting, because flirting with humiliation is all part of his kink. If you ever left a comment, I'm afraid he probably jerked off to it. If you said, 'There's no way a man could ever fit an arm-sized dildo up there,' then he *definitely* grunted and splooged all over his hand.

For a while there, Peggy had what he called a 'hall of fame' on his phone, which was a folder of screenshots of his favourite TikTok comments. I presented him with a cap with the slogan 'Who is Peggy Sue?', which I'm pretty sure he'll never leave the house in. He said it was weird to get a gift from me that wasn't designed to go up his ass, but I reckon he could wedge it up there if he tried.

On our first booking, we met at my usual hotel. He'd come straight from work and was suited up. He wasn't conventionally attractive, and the fact that he was so deferential just cemented that for me. When we started having sex, he told me – a bit too casually – that he enjoys a bit of pain. It started small. He asked me to squeeze his balls and dig in my nails. Then to punch him in the balls. And then he came right out and asked me to punch him in the face. That was harder than you might imagine, because I wasn't angry and he just seemed like a nice guy.

'You're joking,' I said. But he was deadly serious. I slapped him a few times, but then he persuaded me to close my fist. I have to admit the money persuaded me, too, as these hijinks fell under the category of 'kink', which commands an additional $6000 per booking.

'That's not hard enough. *Harder.*'

By the time we were done, I had sweat running down my sides and he was covered in red marks. I'm surprised the people in the adjoining rooms didn't call the front desk. Or maybe they did.

He didn't ask for a pegging in that first session, either because he was too shy or because he understood the power of building up to a full fantasy. Peggy had watched hundreds of hours of my porn, but his favourite video was one where I was vigorously fucking a girl with a strap-on. He immediately wished he was that lucky girl. He asked me to dress up like a bad-ass next time.

I excelled in drama at school, so I don't mind putting on a character. I have leather outfits and knee-high boots, but becoming a dom doesn't come naturally because I'm more of a sub myself. When I get these types of requests I start getting in the right mindset in the Uber journey over, thinking about what I'm going to say the moment I walk in and what kind of inventive punishments I can come up with. As soon as I get to the door, I've got to be *on*, or the illusion is ruined.

Peggy Sue is wired different. He's the only person I've been with who can cum without jerking off, penetrating or being orally stimulated. He could actually go hands-free if I'd built up the tension enough; literally me yelling at him would be the final straw and he'd shoot all over his chest.

The next time I saw him, he asked me to bite down hard on his cock and grind my teeth together, which I have to admit I found incredibly satisfying and animalistic. His cock wasn't even soft – it was rock hard – so you'd think I would be doing some damage. My nose and mouth were filled with the hot metallic scent of blood, and Peggy Sue said it felt like my teeth were almost touching, as though his cock would just pop at any second. He compared it to pinching a hose closed so that the pressure builds up. Then when he came, the pleasure and pain made it the most intense experience imaginable. I was just relieved when he came because I'd been having intrusive thoughts about biting the head of his cock clean off.

It wasn't until the end of that second session that he told me about his desire to be pegged. He'd never experienced it before but he'd been thinking about it for a long time, engaging in more and more auto-ass play. In his early twenties, Peggy was pretty vanilla, but then he met a woman who liked clubbing as much as him and they started to go partying all the time. After one night on the piss, finishing with shots at the bar, they staggered back home and started having sex. The woman conked out on top of him, right in the middle of the act, so he rolled her off and tucked her in – but that left him with the problem of a raging erection. Peggy spotted the wine bottle on the bedside table and suddenly felt butterflies in his stomach. The urge to push it into his body was overwhelming, perhaps even more so knowing that his friend could wake up and be completely disgusted. To his credit, he did go into the lounge room, where he went through half a bottle of lube easing the neck of the wine bottle up his ass. It felt as good as he had suspected. The next day, hungover, just thinking about that secret periodically made him hard.

While I'd pegged girls on film before, I'd never pegged a guy, so the idea got my novelty-seeking brain pumping. He gave me a big chunk of change to go out and buy a strap-on and harness, to surprise him. We hit a hitch early on when it took me about twenty minutes to figure out how to fit the harness. It was seriously eating into our booking time, but he didn't want to help me because I was supposed to be the boss bitch here, and part of that was knowing what the fuck I was doing.

Pegging is actually pretty exhausting. Peggy would be instructing me on my hip action, telling me I needed to be more of a weapon. I'd tell him to shut up and peg him harder. And on and on it went. We never had straight sex anymore. Once, he was late to a booking and I punished him by making him eat his own cum. He was lying jackknifed, with his legs either side of his head, as I penetrated his ass and jacked him off. He came so hard that he wound up blowing a cum bubble out of his mouth.

Over the months I made many visits to the sex shop to buy bigger and bigger strap-ons. We even tried Girthmaster's replica cock, but that didn't fit. Still, Girthy found it hilarious when I told him. We'd gone out to lunch and I gave him the tea on this client who was obsessed with him. I mean, Peggy had absolutely grilled me on how it felt to take a cock as big as Girthy's and whether I was in pain. I could tell he was keen to have the same experience, but Girthy himself wasn't about to volunteer. Instead, I told Peggy he needed to get an anal training kit, which would have different sizes of butt plugs. Within a couple of months he was able to take on the Girthmaster replica. I'm so proud of him.

Other times, I'd get creative and go to hardware and homeware stores to find presents for Peggy. Candles, tacky statuettes, water bottles ... just no glass or ceramics, or anything else that could shatter. He took delight in seeing objects that *shouldn't* be there inserted into his butt, and I always picked a hotel room with mirrored closets for that reason. Sometimes we'd keep this going for four hours. As I told my TikTok followers, 'If your boss is limping today, now you know.'

What really turned Peggy on was the subversion of being a masculine guy, but a guy who *takes* it. When my followers found out about Peggy and wanted to know about his other fantasies, he admitted to wanting to insert a rugby league football into his ass and to go about his day with no one knowing. He speculated that he might have to lube the ball up while deflated and then inflate it once it was wedged inside him. 'Oh my lord, it'll rearrange some organs,' he groaned. So, yeah, those guys you hear about who wind up in the emergency room because they 'accidentally fell' on a huge object? They are all Peggy Sue. And they probably enjoyed the humiliating process of removal just as much as shoving it up there in the first place. Peggy *did* once wind up in emergency because he'd managed to inch one end of a crusty old pool noodle up himself and it had snapped and crumbled, requiring surgical extraction. They didn't ask how it happened. I didn't even find out for a while myself. I hadn't heard from him for a bit and thought he'd ghosted me, but I think he just wanted to recover and then tell me about it in person so that he could see my reaction.

Over time I did get more domineering and I found that slapping Peggy was an exhilarating way to spend an evening. Over the course of a year I estimate Peggy spent at least $100,000 getting off in his own special way. He also inspired me to create my own anal training set in collaboration with Vush; a trio of scarlet plugs with T-bar handles so that there's no danger of an emergency room visit.

I don't see Peggy Sue anymore, though the 'Who is Peggy Sue?' merch line lives on. He was a good sport coming on my podcast – with his voice heavily disguised – and he enjoyed all that attention for a while, but then I think it all got a bit much for him. It's for the best, too, because every mainstream interviewer – along with parents at the school gates – has wanted to ask me about him ever since. Don't worry, though: he booked me straight after the podcast recording so he got one almighty last session in, in which I reminded him about every single humiliating thing he'd said while I fucked him in rhythm with my taunts.

As for Peter Dutton, he was once asked in an interview about being Peggy Sue and he weirdly didn't deny it.

Am I glad I got some mileage out of Peggy Sue? Absolutely.

Am I sick to death of his ass? Definitely.

Why So Many Sex Workers Have ADHD

'Checks out.' – Jackson.

'I told you, babe – look at the state of your make-up drawer.' – Eden.

'You always used to leave your cardigan at school, now I think about it.' – Mum.

'You don't believe in that stuff, do you?' – Dad.

When I got my ADHD diagnosis at age thirty it felt like I was the last to know. But if I look at my 'symptoms' through the lens of sex work, it's so obvious. Most sex workers I know either have a diagnosis or are queuing up to get one – it was my bestie, Eden Lux, who was prodding me to get checked out. Some of the hottest names in porn have talked about ADHD: Mia Khalifa, Rebecca More, Lana Rhoades, Stoya, Jewelz Blu and Elly Clutch among them. Having a job where we control the hours we work totally suits our constant shifting between hyperfocus and lethargy. When I'm 'on', I record a burst of custom videos, I go on tour and book a hotel room for rapid-fire appointments,

I schedule a bunch of sexy content for my socials. I make hay while the sun shines, because I know that a slump will swiftly follow any burst of activity.

Like so many other women, the penny didn't drop until I took one of my children to be diagnosed. Katie was six when I took her to a psychiatrist's office on the Goldie. Of course we arrived late because, having time blindness, I'd thought I could get both of us ready to leave the house in five minutes. Then on the drive across town I'd become increasingly freaked out because I thought I was going to run out of petrol. That's a party trick of mine – noticing it's time to fill up the tank and then forgetting all about it two seconds later. Quite frequently on the way to an appointment I'll be stuck on the side of the road, berating myself while I wait for Jackson to show up with petrol: *Why didn't you just get up earlier? Why didn't you stop at the servo at the bottom of the road? It's not like you don't have enough money to fill the tank these days. What the fuck is wrong with you?*

Even though she usually can't sit still on a chair for five seconds, Katie sat like a cherub while I answered the psychiatrist's questions in a flustered, scattergun fashion. The questions made me sad for my daughter, and also sad for me. All the enquiries about her performance at school, about not being able to finish sentences because she has 40,000 things going on in her head, about emotional dysregulation and about the things that easily frustrate her – I could have been describing my six-year-old self.

At primary school I was quiet, but a real daydreamer in class, which was constantly getting me in trouble. I'd only snap out of the fantasy I was in when a teacher yelled my name, at which point I'd have to hiss to my nearest friend: 'What was the question? Help!' My grades were shitty and I doubt my family had high hopes of me leaving Palmy for any kind of dazzling future.

But at high school, I changed. I became a perfectionist, intent on being an A-grade student. And I was. I aced most subjects, particularly science and maths, which I loved. They call it hyperfocus, because when a person with ADHD fixates on certain topics, no amount of calling their name or waving shiny things at them can pull them out. For me, my focus on my grades came close to self-harm. Focusing on studying distracted me from the fact that I had developed an eating disorder. More recently I've hyperfocused on making as much money as possible.

Getting my own diagnosis a few months after Katie got hers felt like a weight lifted off me. Each trait the psychiatrist went through totally reinforced why I'd made the decision to be a sex worker. Play along with me.

Novelty seeking

When you have ADHD you're constantly novelty seeking to boost your dopamine levels. Working in a boring job where you do the same thing all day would never fulfil that need. Sex work is honestly the only thing that I've ever been consistent at because there are so many avenues available to someone who gets bored easily. I'm not just talking about new clients, I'm talking about the fact that I have to keep changing hats, switching up working on social media, recording videos, editing videos, recording a podcast episode, taking business calls, recording collabs, seeing clients, writing a book. Let's not forget beauty maintenance: my perfectionist streak reappears there, as you can appreciate if you've ever seen my nails. The dopamine dump when I'm sent products from brands and I unbox them on camera makes me feel like every day is Christmas.

The novelty seeker in me also loves the idea that every time I go down to the lobby to greet a guy, it will be a surprise. Even when I've scoured a client's photos beforehand, someone always has the potential to be hotter, beefier or richer in the flesh. Unlikely, but possible.

Impulsive spending

Before I got wise and found myself a great accountant and financial advisor who both have experience dealing with sex workers, I spent every cent I earned. I was useless with money because I found it boring, and therefore paid it no attention. I had no idea that I even had to pay tax. So for the first few years I was on OnlyFans and doing collabs, I took trips everywhere, paid for amazing Airbnbs to shoot in and constantly bought people presents. My love language is giving, so I would splurge for family and friends.

Reward-seeking behaviour

Sex, drugs, thrill-seeking – it's all in a day's work for someone with ADHD. One theory is that people with ADHD have reward sensitivity because they have a lower level of dopamine-releasing neurons. That means they actively seek out stimulation from things that increase dopamine, such as high-fat food, sugar, drugs, alcohol, high-risk sex and general risk taking.

Can talk to anyone … including myself

I talk to myself when I'm driving all the time; it's like a Kayla Jade hot-seat interview. Sometimes I'm practising talking to someone else about an intense situation – giving it a run-through before the actual conversation. Sometimes I'm just thinking out loud about something that's giving me anxiety. Other times I'm recounting a story about something hectic that's happened to me, which I guess has been good practice for my TikTok. My mum used to do this all the time, so I guess it's hereditary. My kids have given up asking who I'm talking to. They'll learn in time. This one's great for sex workers, because often we'll have awkward clients with no social skills, which means it's down to us to fill the silence.

Echolalia

This is a freaky one, but neurodivergent people often echo noises that they hear, whether it's a bird or a person. If someone is humming, I'll start humming along without even realising I'm doing it. Or when I'm filming a collab, if the girl makes an 'ooh' sound, I'll have echoed her so fast it sounds like we're psychic. 'Ooh', 'Ahh', 'Give it to me, baby'. We become evil twins. It makes me a good sex worker, because I'm instinctively tuning in to people's frequencies.

Needing validation

I've always loved having an online presence. I was too young for MySpace but I made good use of MSN Messenger and Bebo before progressing to TikTok and OnlyFans. Seeking validation is actually super handy if you're going to start out on OnlyFans. If you're not thirsty for posting thirst-trap photos, how are you going to keep up the consistency needed to grow on the platform?

Managing my ADHD is a work in progress. When I see a lot of clients my mental health declines, because I make so much of myself available for them. It's draining. My main challenge is keeping organised, especially with time blindness. If you've ever heard a person with ADHD say 'I'm just …' you'll know what I mean. You could be heading out of the door together and they'll 'just' find a whole bunch of things to quickly do first. I also still tend to leave things till the last minute, but I find that pressure spurs me on. I use the calendar in my phone, my manager sends me reminders, and I take my meds.

Sushi Girl

Before she came to see me, Louise had gone to ridiculous lengths to feel a woman's touch. She was a TV producer who frequently flew from Melbourne to Sydney for work. While in Sydney, she'd always treat herself to a massage from one of the many parlours in the city. It was the sort of luxury she wouldn't think of when at home, but it had become a ritual interstate.

It was on one of these visits, as she was lying on her front and zoning out to whale song, that the masseuse skimmed Louise's vulva. Louise froze. She was wearing her underwear, so she assumed it had been a mistake – a stray finger – and she started to relax again. Then the woman began to knead the top of Louise's thighs. Ordinarily, a masseuse would move up the legs and onto the glutes, but this woman was pressing her fingertips over and over into the crease of Louise's butt, dangerously close to her pussy.

Louise started to panic. She should say something. But what? Would the woman be insulted? She lay there, breathing heavily, as the masseuse continued her minute movements. With Louise only able to look through the face hole of the massage table, the woman was distilled into a pair of disembodied hands, roaming around.

Louise, I don't need to tell you, began to get really turned on. The towel lining the face hole began to get damp with her drool as she lay very, very still, all her attention focused on the tops of her thighs.

Abruptly, the woman stopped kneading that zone and instead pushed down hard on the top of Louise's glutes. To Louise's delight and horror, she started to cum. The upward movement of tension, suddenly directed downward, created some kind of orgasmic chain reaction. She bit onto the towel as she ground her clit into the table and moaned.

The moment she finished cumming it was as though a spell had been broken. The masseuse briskly moved to Louise's back and continued the massage. But she *must* have noticed. *Surely* it was deliberate. But Louise had paid upfront!

Louise exited the parlour that day on shaky legs and immediately called her boyfriend to tell him what had happened. He wasn't as excited as she had expected. But, for Louise, that experience marked the beginning of an epic quest: to always seek out a happy ending.

On Louise's next trip to Sydney, the first thing she did after checking in to her hotel and showering was return to the same massage parlour. She felt sheepish as she walked in. Would the staff look at her knowingly and guess what she'd come for? As it turned out, she would leave disappointed. The enterprising masseuse from her previous visit wasn't working, and the massage she received was skilful but uneventful.

The next day she tried another parlour. And then another. Each time, the masseuse kept things above board. Louise found herself jumping on trains further and further out into the inner west, seeking parlours with suspiciously sleazy-looking neon signs or windows blocked by dark blinds.

Louise ordered oily massages, 'exotic' massages and four-hand massages, always making a point of asking if she should keep her underwear on or take it off? Her butt-quaking experience was never repeated. Louse started to get angry. Why was it men could confidently receive a rub and tug, but not a woman? But, then, she couldn't bring herself to ask for anything 'extra' outright, so why would a masseuse even assume that was what she wanted? Maybe she was just a freak, kidding herself that she was on a righteous mission of gender equality.

Over cocktails she filled in a gay friend of hers, bemoaning the fact that she couldn't recreate the experience. 'Just ask,' he said in amazement. He'd been to a bathhouse that very lunchtime, and he knew well that if you don't ask, you don't get.

'You don't understand,' Louise lamented. 'A woman can't just ask.'

Louise's massage mission came to a screeching halt on one trip to Sydney when she ate dinner with colleagues, then excused herself to go back to her hotel. Instead she wandered the length of the street and found a likely-looking joint – neon sign, darkened windows and a hand-printed sign with the promise of 'very relaxing'. Louise tentatively pushed open the door and was immediately greeted by a woman in her fifties who ushered her in as though she should absolutely be there. After paying $120, Louise was directed into a small room and told to get undressed. The woman disappeared. The room, Louise noted, had a mirror lining the wall lengthways. Her pulse quickened. She was clearly in the right place.

Louise was still undressing when a nervous-looking younger woman hurtled through the door as if she'd been pushed. Louise tried to greet her, but the woman said nothing in return. With Louise settled on the table, staring at the floor through the face hole as though it would deliver all the answers to her unasked questions, the woman started to timidly press Louise's shoulder blade.

After fifteen minutes of this, the woman still hadn't strayed from the safe haven of Louise's upper-left quadrant. She was clearly terrified, perhaps not even trained to give a basic massage, let alone to know how to deal with a woman wanting more. Louise felt terrible. It had never even occurred to her that in seeking out massage parlours for sexual activity she could be contributing to sex trafficking. In what she had thought was a feminist quest to receive the same benefits that men do, she had inadvertently put another woman through the wringer. She sat up on the table.

'That's okay,' she said brightly. 'That's enough now.'

'No, no,' the woman said, alarmed. She looked as though she was getting into trouble.

'No, that's okay,' Louise repeated, pulling on her clothes. 'I've got to go actually.'

She squeezed past the masseuse and headed for the front door, never so relieved to be heading out into torrential rain.

Briskly heading to the station, Louise realised she'd have to accept it. She wasn't going to get her happy ending this way.

~

Hardly any women book me as a sex worker. Maybe they feel scared because there's so much stigma around women and sexuality, and they probably also worry that I'd be offended or repulsed. In which case, they can't have watched many of my collabs. I've very enthusiastically eaten pussy, fucked girls with strap-ons and wrangled double-ended dildos. Admittedly I've had way more girl-girl experiences through collabs with other OnlyFans creators than I've had organically in real life, but I've enjoyed them all. Honestly, I'd do it more in my personal life, but most of my hot friends *are* OnlyFans creators, so why wouldn't we film it and make a buck at the same time?

I love it when a woman does bite the bullet and contact me, usually after shyly ogling me on TikTok. Even though I can't show much flesh – there's literally AI that looks for a certain percentage of skin in videos to find accounts to be shut down – I do always try to be sensuous, leaning into the camera, maybe drawing attention to my lips by putting on lipstick, and talking in a low voice.

I love feminine energy. Sex with a woman is more sensual. It's softer and there's more play. It's just more *intimate* than sex with a man. You kiss longer and deeper. You caress rather than slap. You undulate rather than manoeuvre. So I was very happy when Louise messaged me and told me her story. I couldn't stop laughing at that massage mission. It's just the sort of thing I would have done back in New Zealand, trying to titillate myself with some kind of adventure. Louise said that she'd eventually come to the conclusion that what she really wanted to explore was the touch of a woman, and that this desire had been hiding behind the 'safer' front of wanting a happy ending to prove her point that the privilege shouldn't be limited to guys.

Humans are funny.

I booked her in.

~

Louise was tall and slender, with slightly anxious brown eyes and dark blonde hair scraped back into an elaborate knot. She was dressed neatly, favouring moderately expensive, neutral-toned basics. I greeted her warmly in the hotel lobby, giving her a quick hug and light kiss on the cheek as though we were old friends. I think the woman on reception would have been quite confused: she'd seen me many times here before, but never with a nervous fawn.

Presumably thinking it less terrifying to stick with what she knew, Louise had ordered a 'sexy massage'. She'd given me very specific instructions beforehand by text, presumably being too shy to say the words out loud. The text messages spelled out the steps to the unexpected happy ending she'd got all those months ago in Sydney, to the letter. Upper thighs first, for an achingly long time, then the ass.

I counted out Louise's money, which she got a kick out of. She told me that paying for sex felt unexpectedly powerful – not because there was an uneven power dynamic between us, but because she was a woman very forthrightly deciding what she wanted and also eliminating any misunderstandings by paying for it. For a lot of women, sex feels like a transaction of sorts – like sometimes it's expected in return for certain favours a guy has provided. She loved the transparency and simplicity of paying a sex worker for a service on her terms.

Despite that, I noticed she was in the shower for a long time, which is always a sign of nerves. It can be more nerve-racking for a body-conscious woman to get naked with another girl because we naturally compare and contrast, even if we're not judging. I *still* get more nervous with another woman and pay even more attention than usual to my grooming.

Eventually, she emerged, slightly pink-cheeked and scented with some delicious lotion. I was already in role-play mode.

'Please strip down to your underwear and lie down here,' I said, holding my hand out to the bed, on which I'd laid some white fluffy towels. Obediently, she lay on her front, resting her face on her arms and closing her eyes. I'd set some ylang-ylang massage oil on the bedside table and I started warming it in my hands. I straddled Louise and started on her neck and shoulders. I thought she should be legitimately relaxed before we got down to business.

Louise had smooth, pale skin, which on the Gold Coast is a sign of a workaholic. I caressed her curves in long, fluid strokes, and I felt her muscles tense and relax under my fingertips. Eventually I worked down to the base of her spine and I moved to kneel on the bed so that I could begin running my hands up her legs. I got into quite a trance working the oil into her upper thighs, each time pausing right at the top to push my thumbs in, dangerously close to her pussy. Louise had stopped breathing. I slowed down my pace and sensuously circled my fingertips, creeping to the very tops of her thighs, just below her butt crack. It was as though I could feel everything Louise was feeling. I mashed my pussy onto the heel of my foot as I knelt over her.

Swapping from fingers to thumbs, I teasingly pushed the base of her butt-cheeks apart with every upwards stroke, exposing her labia. It was a beautiful sight. I was tempted to lean in and lick her pussy right there, but I had my strict instructions. After one last lingering spreading of her pussy, I switched gears and firmly pushed my hands on her butt. I heard a huge intake of breath. I pushed her butt even harder onto the bed to stimulate her clit. Just as she'd described, a tidal wave of energy receded and then crashed through her cunt, causing her to cry out.

As Louise recovered, laughing helplessly, I lay next to her, propping myself up on one elbow and smiling.

'How was that?' I asked.

'Incredible,' she said. 'But what about you?'

'Oh, I enjoyed it too, don't you worry.'

'But do you want to cum?' She looked shy again. 'I'd *like* it if you came. Would you be able to squirt?'

Like any conscientious high-achiever, Louise had done her homework and would have known full well that hosing the room was my forte. There's nothing subtle about squirting, so I chose the Hitachi Magic Wand, which has to be plugged into the wall. It's loud as hell, but that's all part of the performance.

I propped up two pillows and lay back with my legs spread. I licked a finger and played with one of my nipples as I worked the wand on my pussy. My mind wandered to the time I taught another client to squirt. I'd eased a small vibrator in her butt and slowly fucked her with that as I licked her pussy. Beforehand I'd got her to drink a clear electrolyte drink so that she would feel confident in just letting go. A lot of women worry that squirting is just piss, but if they feel sure that the liquid will be clear anyway, they're more likely to relax. Sure enough, it was like a dam burst. She was crying with joy and I felt like a midwife who'd just delivered something magical into the world. Reliving her screaming orgasm now, I got myself to the brink and pulled the wand away just in time to let Louise see me cum; a waterfall of liquid raining down on the towel.

That was unusually thoughtful of me. I've drenched many a hotel bed, and it just so happened this time that my efforts to create a semi-realistic setting saved the day.

~

The second time I saw Louise, a few months later, she warned me not to eat beforehand. When I met her in the lobby she was weighed down with two plastic bags full of sushi and sashimi that it turned out she'd made herself. Maybe spending all those hours labouring in the kitchen over fiddly sheets of seaweed and delicate cuts of salmon just added to the build-up.

Louise had always had a secret fetish for *nyotaimori*, which is the act of eating food off the body of a naked woman. *Nyotaimori* reached its peak of popularity in the 1980s with Japanese salarymen. The woman must lie completely still and silent while the men pluck raw fish from her vulva and presumably talk shop, reducing the woman to a prop. Louise said she'd always wanted to have someone eat sushi off her body and she always figured the diner would be a man, before one day her mind, unbidden, inserted a woman into her fantasy. Are you sensing a theme here? I am.

Louise had carefully waxed her body and washed with non-scented soap. She lay down on the bed naked and I arranged the food over her body (no wasabi, obviously), watching in fascination as tiny muscles quivered at my touch. Truthfully, the scenario was awkward. I didn't know what I should say throughout. In Japanese *nyotaimori* there would be multiple people talking over and completely ignoring her, plus I couldn't speak Japanese and wasn't about to attempt an accent and risk being cancelled. I settled on the odd '*Mmm*' as I plucked slithers of sashimi from her belly. I'm a germaphobe, though, so the experience tested me. File under: nice idea.

Keen to wrap this part of the procedure up and get to what I know best, I started deliberately dragging the tips of the chopsticks over her body, gradually getting lower until I reached her pussy and skimmed her clit. I could tell Louise was ready to ditch the soy sauce and let me properly dine out on her pussy. Because she was so sensitive to touch, I'd brought along a vibrator shaped like a feather with a delicate tip. Designed for tickling the clit and labia, when combined with a tongue the effect is curiously like warm liquid running on the cunt. Highly recommended, FYI.

While she wasn't about to meet my eyes, looking up I could see Louise's stomach muscles tauten, and sensed she was close. I flicked my tongue at her clit while running the tip of the feather around her pussy hole and her whole body shuddered. Her hips pulled away from me and she came. I only gave her time to laugh – a cute Louise signature – before I went in again, positive she had more in her. This time she came immediately, pushing my head into her cunt. Good girl.

These are the times my job is the most rewarding. I never saw Louise again, but without wanting to take *all* the credit, I felt like I'd set her on a new path of self-discovery. I wish more women would get brave and explore their desires with me. Women overthink trying sex with another woman. They worry they're gay, or wonder if they should be gay, to legitimately initiate things. To me, it's simple. If you own a pussy and you like it being gently touched, why wouldn't you want to? Maybe it's finding a play partner that worries them most – like they'd either have to string along a woman who is gay-all-the-way or risk jeopardising a friendship. So, ladies, your friendly neighbourhood sex worker is always happy to help.

My recipe for eating pussy well

Firstly, and most importantly, there's no formula. Your guide is the woman's breath. If it's getting deeper, or if she's almost holding it, you're on the right track. Not all women will give vocal cues – be that words or moans – but in time you'll learn to read those breaths and undulations.

Take it super slow. I love dipping two fingers and slowly fucking a woman while I lick her clit. If you have toys, I suggest using something delicate first. By teasing the outside of her pussy you can do away with lube, which can get messy when you're trying to eat a girl out.

Some women love it when you stretch the pussy wide, as though a cock is in there. It means there's friction on the clit from the clitoral hood, but also, the feeling of being really exposed can turn some women on.

Many women aren't used to asking for what they like, so I'll get really specific on her behalf. 'Should this be softer or harder?' 'Flat tongue or pointed?' 'Do you want a toy inside you?'

Lastly, don't be afraid to go for seconds. After the initial peak, many women still have a lot of energy built up and could easily let go again. You'll know when they're really done because they'll shove you away like they've just been electrocuted.

Easy-peasy.

Dude, Go Home

Have you ever had a dream where you've made out with someone you don't know well, then you wake up and that weird intimacy has stayed with you all day? That's what sex work is like. You're left with the ghostly impression of a client – their lips at your neck, their hands on your hips, their cock at the back of your throat – and you can't just scrub it off in the shower.

But I try.

Sex work can be fun. It can be exciting. It lights up my novelty-seeking brain like a Christmas tree. But it's also death by a thousand cuts. For every good guy, there are ten scumbags who make you lose faith in the whole gender.

There's the guy who had known me since I was six and subscribed to my OnlyFans. The old classmate who messaged me to say he'd seen my videos on Pornhub. The man who yanked my hair so hard during doggy, not a day after I'd made a video talking about how I was worried I was going bald. The clients who play mind games and make you ask for the money, even though they've seen hundreds of sex workers before you and they know full well they should have it ready.

Some guys don't want to fuck, they just want to pull themselves off while they listen to you talk dirty. Maybe you've seen *Sex, Lies, and Videotape*, the 1989 movie about James Spader, a sex addict who films women talking about their fantasies, but never fucks them. That might sound like the dream client, but no: it's actually more exhausting coming up with some bullshit fantasy (never real – that's none of their business) that casts them as the star.

And I get so mad at the guys who think that, in addition to sucking their cock, I should listen to them bitch about their ex-partners. Or the clients who swear they're not seeing anyone but then a few bookings later they've forgotten their backstory and are moaning about how their wife never comes along when they're coaching their kid's soccer game.

Another *bah-baaaah* are the guys who insist they're XL and spend a lot of time before a booking warning me about the hectic dimensions of their schlong, hyping it up like they're packing a foot-long Subway. I don't bother packing XL condoms for those ones, because they've outed themselves as someone with an average-sized dick. I remember one such booking where I met the guy in the lobby and we took the lift up together. I'm 163 centimetres and I noted that we were eye to eye in height. Nothing wrong with that, but I wondered if being on the shorter side made him desperate to prove he could overcompensate with his cock. He'd told me that a regular rubber would cut off his circulation.

Once we were ready to rock, I looked at his cocktail wiener. *Hmm. Maybe it's a grower*, I thought. *Give him some time.* He rolled on an XL franger that he'd brought with him, and we settled into missionary. All good, until he pulled out to change position. The condom was nowhere to be seen. I reached down and found it half hanging out of me.

'I'll grab a regular,' I said, reaching for the bedside table.

'No, no, it'll cut off my circulation.'

Jesus, what do you do? I made out like I was getting one of his XLs, but swapped it last minute for a regular. It fitted like a glove.

'You love this big cock, don't you?' he said, as he apparently pumped me from behind. Part of me didn't want to boost his ego any more, but he was paying handsomely, so I told him I did indeed love it.

I wish guys knew that I'm not actually that eager for a big cock. The last thing you'd want to do on an eight-hour work day is sit on a baseball bat, right? At least I was able to persuade this guy that I couldn't take a facial because with a cock that big I'd surely drown.

At this point, you might be thinking, yes, Kayla, we all have our fair share of experiences of men being less than legendary ... so let me up the ante.

Role-play probably sounds like a relatively harmless activity on a booking. Turns out, it depends who's asking. One man wanted me to role-play being his step-daughter. Another, his girlfriend's best friend. Of course, I put them through hell for even asking and tell them what a bad person they are, but it's yet another blow to my wellbeing. One man asked me if I'd come to his house and suck off his dog. Another wanted me to say degrading racial slurs. I turned up to one booking and discovered it was a photographer who I'd had to block on every platform for stalking me.

Some clients are practised boundary-pushers who want to coerce an unsure new girl into doing bareback (no condom), or doing anal, or doing him and his friends at the same time. I'm super clear in my messages that bareback is *not* an option, yet I'll occasionally have a booking where the guy pressures me and complains about it the entire session. Yeah, sure. I'll risk my health for your fifteen minutes of extra pleasure. Other guys will be snorting lines (which I never join them in; for all I know they could be spiking me with ketamine) and then they can't perform because they've got coke dick, so they want money off.

So often, when the hotel door shuts behind us, I'm in fight-or-flight mode. Often, I'm thinking: *Just get through this, just get through this.* As soon as bookings like that are done I'm out the door like a lightning bolt. When there's a bad energy I become super aware that there are only the two of us in the room and things could turn bad in a heartbeat, so I can't lose my cool.

Women are always asking me if I ever fake an orgasm during bookings. Yes, of course I do, and I don't think a client has ever even mentally questioned its authenticity. Sex work actually diminishes my libido. So many men can't even kiss properly. It's like they're stunted at schoolyard level or they're trying to spell their name with their tongue. Don't get me started on them giving oral.

Most of the men who come to see me don't know how to have a basic conversation. They'll say some weird shit and I'll think, *Do you not have any filter?* Maybe Newbie Kayla would feel sorry for them, but not anymore. I just act my little heart out, because it's a business transaction. If you're in hospitality, customer service or sex work, it's your job to be amenable. When I'm feeling dark, I can feel disgusted at even the nicest or blandest guy.

The Celebrity Cuck

They say never meet your idols – you'll only be disappointed. The A-Lister had been on posters tacked to my wall in Palmerston North when I was young, gazing down at me with an inscrutable expression. Now I had been airdropped into his world (first class, of course) and the insanity of it all was making my head spin.

The WhatsApp message had come from my friend Troy, an LA-based adult performer who I'd appeared in some scenes with and had a mega crush on. He told me the A-Lister was a fan and wanted to fly me to Greece to party for a few days. Troy would be there, too, and a bunch of other people, basically just being the A-Lister's friends for hire during his Mediterranean holiday. I had to sign a hefty non-disclosure agreement, of course. I'd seen a few NDAs, but this particular one ran for about thirty pages, making it crystal clear that I could stand to lose about five times my usual annual earnings if I ever gave away the Disclosing Party's identity. I tried to picture his lawyer drawing up this agreement with the knowledge of what was likely to go down, and wondered if he was anything like my lawyer: terse, conservative but with a twinkle in his eye that suggested he knew how to keep a secret and had heard them *all*.

Within a few days of signing, I was on a plane to Greece. I hadn't spoken to the A-Lister yet, only his team. I was literally shaking at Athens International Airport, wondering if whoever was picking me up would human-traffic me somewhere beyond my control.

Thankfully, Troy was already at the hotel, so we went out to dinner the night before we were due to party. As I said, I had quite a crush on Troy. He was laidback and reliable, and quick to crease up into a beautiful smile. He was one of the industry's good guys. Troy had been the hired schlong at quite a few celebrity events, and he suspected this would be a freak-off of epic proportions. No one had told me yet if I was there just for the vibe or for sex, but we decided it was safe to assume it was the latter. We went back to Troy's room and fucked for hours, to get us both into the right headspace.

The next morning we met the driver outside the hotel and made the long trip through the winding hills, thankful for the air-conditioning that was on full blast. Now that I was with Troy, my nerves had turned to excitement. I was in some of the most beautiful countryside I'd ever seen, and I knew that when I got there it would be a game of spot-the-celebrity.

The car dropped us outside the courtyard of what was modestly called 'the villa' but looked more like a palace to me. At this point, I realised I hadn't got the memo. Everyone gathered in the courtyard was wearing black, while I was dressed in a bright blue dress. At least I looked snatched.

I took Troy by the hand and led him towards the bar at speed. En route, a waiter crossed my path, so I whisked two champagnes from his tray, handed them to Troy and carried on to the bar to order tequila shots. It was Clase Azul, smooth as silk. I ordered two more and after that it was easier to chat. Everyone looked vaguely familiar, but I swear I have facial blindness, so I couldn't with 100 per cent confidence think, *Oh, okay, you're from* that *TV show*, or *You're* that *producer*. In between conversations I nipped inside to find the bathroom, my eyes taking a moment to adjust from the bright sunlight. The nearest bathroom was as big as a master bedroom, decked out in marble and gold. I checked myself in the mirror. My eyes looked huge. I applied some more lip gloss from my bag, took a few deep breaths and went back out.

I could see that the A-Lister and his wife were mingling, but I avoided eye contact to give them their space. Eventually, though, we drifted closer and Troy introduced me. The Wife regarded me impassively as the A-Lister took my hand and shook it – or, rather, held it limply for a moment. I looked into those distinctive eyes that had stared down at me from my bedroom wall and it was a truly surreal moment. He didn't even look any older. The A-Lister said that they both loved my work, at which point the Wife gave a tight smile, and then we just danced and vibed in our little group. I noticed the A-Lister wasn't drinking, but still, he was singing along to the choruses. And when he sang, everyone sang.

A couple of songs in, I pulled Troy closer and French-kissed him. Even though I knew everyone's eyes were on us, making out always made me feel more relaxed and in control. We were deep into it when I felt a tap on my shoulder. It was a member of the A-Lister's team, a huge unit who I'll call Benny.

'He wants you to go upstairs,' Benny said, unsmiling. Looking around, I realised that the A-Lister and the Wife had left the scene.

Troy and I followed Benny inside. There was a massive staircase on either side of the foyer, and Benny started trudging up the right side, so we trailed behind him, trying not to laugh. By now I was buzzing from the tequila shots and excited by the idea of getting sexy. I dragged my fingertips along the flock wallpaper of the long hallway, checking out the vases and statues that were probably worth more than my year's takings.

The bedroom was more like a penthouse suite, with its own kitchen and bathroom, and its centrepiece was a massive bed that could probably 'sleep' about ten people. The Wife was already settled in the middle of it, completely naked, with that famous body even more eye-popping in real life. The A-Lister came out of the bathroom in a robe, flopping down in an armchair.

'You guys have sex,' he said, gesturing at me and Troy, as though he was just asking a waiter for more breadsticks.

Troy and I exchanged looks and then started undressing each other. The A-Lister and the Wife were watching intently as I took Troy's big cock in my mouth. I was glad for how familiar he felt in these weird-ass surroundings. I tried to block out the eyes on me and just focus on my technique. After a while we swapped positions so that Troy could bury his face in my pussy. Looking up at the scalloped ceiling, I tried to think tactically. Were we really just here to put on a show, or were we supposed to be involving the couple who had paid for it all? As Troy went to town I opened my legs wider so that one knee touched the Wife. Would she respond? A moment passed, then I saw an almost imperceptible nod from the A-Lister. The Wife stroked my inner thigh.

'I want to watch you fuck my husband,' she said.

Troy pulled away from my pussy and retreated to a discreet distance on the bed. This was it – I was about to fuck the A-Lister, who was dropping his robe to the floor and walking towards me, his cock at half-mast. He had a mid-sized dick, nothing special, but I lavished attention on it like it was the most impressive specimen I'd ever seen. I used both my hands as I gave him head, to give the impression of it being hard to handle.

The A-Lister was pretty lacklustre, which didn't improve any once he started fucking me. He pulled on a condom and pumped me rhythmically from behind, staring down at my ass like he was reading his phone. I started throwing back, to try to beef up the show. You'd think that someone who has fucked thousands of beautiful women would have an A game, but maybe it was all meaningless to him by then. He finished within about five minutes. He did tell me I had the best pussy, which I tried not to seem too pleased about in front of the Wife.

I had assumed that the Wife would be next in line, but then Benny started making out like it was his turn, trying to touch me and get on the bed. It pissed me off, because he'd treated Troy and me with such disdain when he summoned us to follow him earlier, like we were the shit on his shoe. Now he was acting with total entitlement, as if I had no choice but to comply.

'Nuh-uh, buddy,' I said, trying to keep it light. I stood up and started pulling on my panties. I wanted another tequila and I wanted Troy to come with me, stat. Benny kept on at me the whole time I was trying to shimmy into my dress, cursing at how tight it was. The A-Lister and the Wife just watched, seemingly bored.

'Mate, the answer's no,' I said through gritted teeth. I finally got the dress on and stepped into my shoes, but Benny followed me out of the room and down the stairs.

'You gonna fuck me, bitch?' he said. 'What, you too good?'

At the bottom of the stairs, Troy swung around and stepped between me and Benny.

'Back off, dude,' he said. 'She said no. Fuck off and chill.' Benny shoved Troy on the shoulder, and Troy shoved back, with both hands, hard. People started gathering around us in interest, like this was a colosseum, not an overpriced fuck pad. Benny threw a punch and Troy reciprocated. They hit the marble floor and for a while they were a blur of Balenciaga.

'*Fuck!*' I said. I was scrambling for my phone, opening the Uber app. 'Come on, Troy, let's just get of here.'

I managed to get Troy outside but the Uber was twenty minutes away because we were in the middle of nowhere. Now that the tequila buzz was wearing off, I was on edge, waiting for Benny's big fat head to emerge again. Just as the car arrived, Benny came back out, this time with some buddies.

'[The A-Lister] wants another round with her,' he said, locking eyes with Troy, even though he was talking about *me* and my body. 'You gotta stay.'

I looked at Troy. He knew the rules of these situations better than I did ... but surely they couldn't literally force us to stay and have sex?

'We're leaving, dude,' Troy said firmly, opening the car door for me.

'You're going to regret that,' Benny said. But we were out of there.

Troy and I wound up blowing off steam back at the hotel, raiding the mini bar and fucking all night. It was like we'd just had a trauma bonding experience. And we were on holiday, after all.

~

The next morning at breakfast, Troy got a call from the A-Lister. I leaned across the table to try to hear, convinced we were in big trouble, but he seemed super chill about it all. He hadn't seen the commotion and he apologised for any misunderstandings ... but wouldn't we come back over to the 'villa' again today? We could leave whenever we wanted to. Troy looked at me and I shrugged. We'd actually had fun apart from our run-in with Benny, and apparently he wasn't going to be there. Okay, we agreed. We'd be there in a few hours.

This time around, the A-Lister greeted us personally when the driver dropped us off. He said everyone was hanging out by the pool and he'd take us. I swear to god, it was a fifteen-minute walk around the property to the pool. I was racking my brain wondering what to talk about, since we had absolutely nothing in common and I didn't want to fan-girl by outright flattering him. Even though the A-Lister was being chill, all I could get out of him was vague talk of a few projects he had on the go and the fact that there were some girls he really wanted me to meet.

Like everything else in this place, the pool was oversized. In fact, it seemed like the whole of last night's party had just relocated inside it. A lot of girls were swimming naked and he told me I should join them, so I stripped off and lowered myself in. Conversation is always superficial in this kind of scenario. You just rely on alcohol to get you through, though I noticed that the A-Lister still wasn't drinking, and – unusually – I hadn't seen any drugs doing the rounds, either. I think the guy's too much of a control freak to indulge, preferring to just direct everyone in his own kind of weird movie.

As I bobbed around in the pool I took full advantage of the circulating waitstaff, drinking a few cocktails in quick succession. The sun was oppressively hot, so I alternated between baking naked on the lounge chairs and jumping back in. A sketch artist scuttled over to draw us girls whenever we reclined on the chairs. The recording of the event was very much a one-way street. Even though we were allowed to keep hold of our phones, there was barely any reception and it had been made very clear by the A-Lister's team that we were under no circumstances allowed to film or take photos. The A-Lister himself liked to document everything, not just through the artist but through a photographer and videographer he had doing the rounds. Each time the videographer came by I smiled and waved, giving some variation of how much I loved to fuck. All the other girls were statuesque, which was obviously the A-Lister's type. One Amazonian woman was only wearing black masking tape, which curved around her ass and titties so that they defied gravity.

I stuck close to two super-nice girls like they were my security blanket. These girls were in stark contrast to some of the models from Miami, who showed up together and immediately started acting like they were above everyone else. In particular, the models were shitty with the waitstaff, which is a huge no-no for me. When the A-Lister came over with the Wife, they immediately perked up and started flirting with him. *This is dumb*, I thought. When invited to hang out with a couple there's an unspoken law: pay more attention to the wife. If you fawn over the husband, particularly the more-famous husband, you risk pissing her off. It's not that delicate a dance, honestly. I just make it a rough 70/30 split of my attention: her/him. These Miami girls were laughing at everything the A-Lister said and I suspected their cards were marked. If we'd been in a royal court in the olden days, the Wife would have had their heads. Even though her husband was a powerful man, I got the vibe that she wore the pants. At one point, she saw him on his phone and literally snatched it from him. 'Who are you messaging?' she said with a sour expression, but whoever it was, she found no answer on the screen.

Someone called dinnertime, so Troy and I joined the others and headed into the house, most of us still nude. Inside there were chefs and waitstaff not blinking an eye. We were directed into the kitchen, where we could ask them to cook us whatever we wanted. Orders completed, we took our seats outside in a picture-perfect garden, central to which was a long, rustic wooden table with a buffet laid out.

I somehow ended up sitting next to the A-Lister and the Wife. Everyone was craning forward to hear his wildly indiscreet stories – the guy has obviously never signed an NDA himself. As we ate, we showed each other funny TikToks and made superficial chit-chat, all getting on just fine. The A-Lister had a reputation for being moody and difficult, but I was seeing a much lighter side to him.

After dinner, the music cranked up higher and I started dancing on the table with my two new besties. One of the girls noticed a waiter surreptitiously filming us from the second floor, and I saw one of the A-Lister's team members bolt up there. The waiter was fired on the spot and ejected from the house.

It was early evening but I knew this party would go on all night. My make-up and hair had been ruined by being in the pool, so Troy and I made the call to freshen up back at the hotel and then return later, recharged.

Three hours passed before we returned, and when our car pulled up we saw the three nasty girls from Miami waiting outside with their bags, with particularly sour expressions on their faces.

'What's going on, guys?' I said, overdoing the concern. It turned out they'd put on a sex show and when one of the other girls leaked a little blood because she had her period, one of the Miami crew told her she was disgusting, at which point the Wife told all three Miami girls it was time to leave. I fully back the Wife on her decision. Those chicks were a walking bummer.

The moment the A-Lister saw me and Troy, he greeted me with a kiss and said, 'Go and see that woman there, she's gonna dress you.' He'd employed a designer who was running up custom outfits for us all. My 'dress' wound up being a bikini, but it fitted perfectly and the designer gave me a beautiful black robe to wear over it. I noticed all the girls were wearing these robes, which seemed a little culty but, like, high-fashion culty. Now that the sun had gone down, the garden was lit up in red and the vibe seemed darker. I stuck close to Troy. There can't have been more than fifty people, but little groups were forming as people had sex and others gathered around them to watch. It was kinda civilised, kinda seedy.

The A-Lister materialised in front of us, his eyes bugging a bit. 'I want you and Troy to have sex,' he said, pointing to a lounger. I find that when you're in a freaky situation, it's best to be the freakiest person there, so I decided to really go for it. We started fucking in front of the A-Lister's celebrity friends, with Troy pulling my hair from behind as he pounded me. I locked eyes with different people as I got shunted back and forth by his cock, relishing the wildness of it all.

The rest of the evening was a blur of fucking. At one point I got involved with a pod of girls who were making themselves squirt. Another time I wandered over to the pool to watch Troy give a star turn fucking two girls. I lost him for an hour, then I spotted him again, this time making up a circle of around ten guys who had gathered around the Wife. I pushed through the crowd of onlookers, the biggest crowd of the evening, and watched in disbelief. The Wife was on her knees, sucking each of the ten dicks in turn. The A-Lister stood on the sidelines, watching.

I realised that, for all the emphasis he tried to put on group sex, the A-Lister's real kink was watching people fuck his wife, which made him a regular cuck. The term 'cuckold' is taken from the female cuckoo's tendency to lay eggs in other birds' nests, and was then applied to men whose partners cheat on them. In kink parlance, it refers to men who like to watch. I think deep down the A-Lister would love to suck a bunch of cocks, but as no NDA could be tight enough to stop that getting out, he has to resort to putting himself in the Wife's shoes. Maybe he's a bit of a germaphobe, too. A lot of celebrities seem to be, as if coming into contact with proles would contaminate their success. I get germaphobia, though. For hygiene reasons I don't want a client's semen anywhere near my face or mouth, and absolutely no spitting, which is some guys' thing. It's so gross. I cannot. When I was shooting porn I occasionally had to do girl-girl-boy scenes where the guy came in the other girl's mouth and then she spat the semen into mine, or vice versa. But if there's no camera rolling? No, thank you.

And now here was the Wife, readying herself to take ten different loads in her mouth. It was a bit much for me. I'd only been there two days but it seemed like a lifetime, as if the real world was just some fever dream becoming more and more eroded from my memory. I needed to get out of there. Troy was obviously otherwise engaged, so I snuck out and asked one of the drivers if he'd take me back to town. Thankfully, this time there was no Benny-shaped hassle.

The A-Lister and his friends would party for days on end with no responsibilities, just flying participants in and out. They curated these freak-offs that required an insane amount of power, because they needed this ramped-up lifestyle just to feel something. Other than these orgies they were stuck in their bubbles, going from private jet to hotel suite to wherever they worked. They could never go out to a restaurant or a shop, and so everyone in their sphere needed to be ever-available. In return, their entourage – the only people they could supposedly trust – were leeches.

Back at the hotel, I got straight onto the airline's website. Having now experienced the A-list lifestyle firsthand, I was going to do whatever it took to bump forward my flight and get back to my darling Z-list fam.

Billion-dollar Baby

Ever since I'd found a few bars of reception my phone hadn't stopped pinging. I had around sixty unread messages and missed calls. When was this guy going to get it? I fired off an SMS, irritated as fuck.

'I have family. I have a life. I have to work. I can't be at your beck and call.'

He replied immediately.

'Where are you? You can't do this to me. You need to get back here NOW.'

When I left Greece, I'd messaged the A-Lister's team to thank them and to let them know that it was too late to summon me back. I was nervous about their response, but no one seemed that fussed. My absence would hardly make a dent in all the pussy they'd imported for the week.

I flew straight to New Zealand because a family member was getting married. After a day's recovery time, I had to fit into a very different kind of party – one where the bride wore white and there were no black robes. It was a relief to see Jackson and the kids, and to return to a sense of normalcy.

After the wedding ceremony we went on to the reception at a vineyard. There wasn't much phone reception but a few hours in I did find a spot where I could check my messages. The A-Lister was irate that I had left the country without his permission. Eventually I managed to calm him down and explain that being on duty with him meant I couldn't be with my kids. It was the right thing to say: the A-Lister abruptly switched from coercive to sweet. He understood. He wished me well. He hoped to see me again sometime. The about-turn made my head spin, but I'd take it.

Several times over the next few months I randomly heard from the A-Lister. He even messaged me from his public Instagram account, which seemed excessively stupid to me – all I'd have to do was screenshot his sexy/needy messages and share them and I'd probably get half a million new followers ... but I guess he liked living on the edge. It was a full year before he actually summoned me again. I was with another client in my usual hotel on the GC when I saw his code name pop up out of the corner of my eye, and made my excuses to check my phone in the bathroom. The A-Lister said he'd just arrived in Singapore, which wasn't a huge trip for me. He'd love to have my company. Just him this time, not the Wife.

I decided to do it for the plot – and for $30,000. Troy wouldn't be able to join me this time, which made me nervous, but I just assumed it would be similar to Greece: lots of girls in the same boat, cocktails, happy days. The A-Lister was typically impatient and wanted me to leave the next morning, so I had to call Jackson and get him to do an evening run to the supermarket and get me some fake tan: not ideal, but it would have to do.

The A-Lister's people transferred money for a business-class seat, but

I booked economy and kept the other $4000 to fly my mum out and treat her after my booking was done. Jackson drove me to the airport and hugged me goodbye, asking me to call as soon as I got to the hotel. I was marinating in that cheap tan the whole flight, but at least I didn't pong out the business-class section – cringe.

I had no visa and no idea if I needed one, but luckily most people in Singapore spoke English so it was at least easy to find my way around the airport and to my hotel. I literally had one hour to do my full glam look before I was due to meet the A-Lister. *His* hotel wasn't even called a hotel, it was called an 'elevated luxury downtown sanctuary', but I had packed a long trenchcoat to try to make myself look more decent. Underneath it was a fishnet tube dress that the A-Lister had specifically requested, having spotted it in one of my videos.

You would never be able to find this 'sanctuary' just by walking down the street. It was so exclusive you had to turn down a nondescript alleyway, get buzzed through a gate and then take a path to the first level, where you'd be greeted by a concierge. Then it was up to the reception proper, on the fortieth floor. It was so artsy and beautiful.

I was sent up to the A-Lister's suite, but it wasn't even him who answered the door. A guy who dressed kinda like him jerked his head, and I followed him into a room that they'd set up as a work station for the week. I don't know how much work they were actually doing, though. The three other guys there seemed to be on site just to agree with the A-Lister whenever something batshit came out of his mouth.

Things had changed. After our initial smooch, I took a seat and was regaled with what I can only describe as narcissistic mumbling and rambling. His ideas didn't sound so brilliant anymore; in fact, they were verging on conspiracy theories. The guys just nodded. 'Word.'

I tried to call a halt to his spiel by moving closer and working my feminine wiles. I'd much rather be reacquainted with his average penis than have to nod along with the boys. I wondered why there were no girls around this time. It made the energy weird. One of his bros kept side-eyeing me, like, *Why are YOU here?* But I was thinking the exact same thing about him.

My tactic worked. By leaning in to the A-Lister and grazing his ear with my lips, I suddenly had his full attention. He pulled me to my feet and started dancing to the music. I didn't know the words, but he sang along to them all, imbuing them with great meaning. Taking things into my own hands, I led him down the hall to what I hoped was a bedroom. Once inside, I knelt on the floor and pulled his cock out of his shorts.

'That's it. Thuck that cock,' he urged me. It was surreal hearing him speak off-duty, because he lost the deep, resonant voice and sounded way more goofy, with a slight lisp.

Then he said it again and added a bigoted slur. I looked up at him.

'You thay it,' he said. 'Call me that.'

'I'm not calling you that,' I said, with a half-laugh, but he was serious. 'No, no, I can't say that.'

I'd never considered that I would have to add a new boundary at this stage in my career, but apparently I did. I didn't have time to consider the psychology of it, though, because he had already moved on to pushing another boundary. He'd slid his cock in my pussy without a condom.

I lay back and let the A-Lister fuck me, my mind doing the maths. I never raw-dogged on the job, ever, but could this time be worth it? Like the immature boy he was, of course he hadn't asked me if I was on the pill. I was, but with the different time-zones I'd passed through lately, had I even remembered to take the last couple?

You could have a billion-dollar baby, I thought to myself, my mind boggling at the potential maintenance he'd be paying.

The A-Lister finished inside me, then pulled out quickly, the last pump of cum splashing my pussy. So, so teenage. Did he really think that was cool? Did he just like living on the edge, even if it wound up costing him a huge chunk of his fortune and his marriage?

I kept a poker face and cooed about how hot that was. The A-Lister plonked down beside me on the bed and video-called the Wife. She wasn't at all fazed by the sight of me.

'You remember Kayla?' The A-Lister said.

'Yeah, hi.'

He didn't mention the no-condom thing.

I pretended not to listen to their chat about his work and reached for my own phone.

~

The A-Lister sent me on a shopping trip to kill a few hours while he worked, giving me an extra $5000 in cash to spend, which I guess was loose change for him. His driver took me to a cool neighbourhood and I found a designer vintage store, picking up a cute Balenciaga handbag that I planned to use that night. Apparently some girls were coming around, which surely meant we were going to hit some clubs. In another store I found four vintage T-shirts for Jackson that cost a couple of thousand dollars because they were so rare. The driver didn't say a word to me on either leg of the trip.

Back at the sanctuary, the girls had showed up and were super friendly. The vibe was much more energetic with them around, and even the A-Lister's friends were lightening up. We got stuck into the tequila – all of us except him.

At around three in the morning, our chorus of trying to persuade him to come to the club raised in volume from teasing to bullying. The A-Lister got mad. He couldn't just go out, he said. He'd need a separate car, and security. In retrospect, I can imagine he gets really paranoid in public, because he can't control the narrative. People would stare, people would approach, people might even come swinging, just so they can say that they did. But at the time, I was buzzed from the booze and tired of his whining. We wanted to go *out*. The tequila had me thinking that he wasn't as relevant anymore as he thought he was. In fact, I was starting to think he was a massive loser. Literally everything he said was giving me the shits. He was so demanding; he sounded like the crazy boy-king in *Game of Thrones*, intent on controlling and punishing everyone around him. I needed to channel some main player energy.

'Well, *I'm* going,' I said. And thank god, when I stood up, the others did too.

That night, I fed the remainder of the cash he'd given me for shopping into the G-strings of girls at the strip club. They were so much more appreciative of my attention than he was. When I awoke the next afternoon, head like a dumpster, I ghosted him for the second time. He got the message. I didn't hear from him again until a week later, when I posted some videos of me shopping in Singapore to feed the content beast.

'Take those down,' he messaged, even though the videos gave no indication that I was there with a client. It was the last command of his I ever obeyed.

Anora Does Shanghai

Days after getting back from Singapore, I was off to China. Sex work is illegal there, but that didn't stop a young rich guy from requesting that I fly over for a two-hour booking. When I looked up Yúzé, I couldn't find out much about him, other than his name meant 'rainfall'. Windfall, more like. This guy had Daddy's money running through his veins. He *had* to have been a billionaire trust-fund kid.

A model I knew had been booked by him and so she referred me, hooking me up with Yúzé's assistant, since Yúzé himself could hardly speak a word of English. That's fair enough – I can only speak one word of Chinese, and that's '*Yóukè! Yóukè!*' – 'Tourist! Tourist!'

Luckily, Shuyi did speak good English and she was really friendly. Still, she was very vague about who Yúzé was. I just knew it would be an easy job and that he was paying. I felt like I was stepping into *Anora*, the 2024 movie about a New Jersey stripper, played by Mikey Madison, who becomes the paid plaything of the son of a Russian oligarch – a twenty-one-year-old who's never worked a day in his life and has more money than sense.

Shuyi transferred me the money for business-class flights and I did my usual trick of booking economy, putting the remainder towards the kids' private school fund. It was a ten-hour overnight flight. I was happy to just put on a face mask, knock myself out and slum it. I've always quite liked economy-class food anyway; there's lots going on with those trays, plenty of little containers to open and keep my ADHD chimp-brain happy.

Before I left, Shuyi had warned me to stay at the hotel. If I had to go out, I should be careful – don't be on my phone and don't take photos, particularly because I might inadvertently be photographing a government building. Basically, she didn't want me to draw any attention to her boss.

As soon as I turned on my phone when I landed in Shanghai I noticed I could still access my social media apps by using data roaming, but I decided not to post a single thing until I got back – even though I would discreetly film bits and pieces. I'd only brought a carry-on case to try to limit my time under airport surveillance, but I was feeling quite paranoid walking through the deluxe airport. I'd dressed down in sweats, with no make-up. Even so, people were staring at me because there's not much you can do to play down a double BBL. I was starting to get a profile as a sex worker and I wondered if the advancements in facial recognition would trigger some mysterious watch list. '*Yóukè! Yóukè!*'

Shuyi had arranged for a driver, who I spotted with relief when I made it through customs. The driver didn't say a word as he eased the limo through traffic. Eventually, we pulled up outside a stunning hotel in downtown Shanghai and I got out, feeling the breeze on my face for what would be the only time in twenty-four hours. Not many of the staff spoke English, but someone showed me up to my suite, where I had the whole afternoon to get ready before Yúzé arrived. Shuyi called to make sure I was settled and recommended that I charge a massage to the room, so I went down to the hotel spa centre and had a lymphatic massage to de-puff myself after the plane journey. Then I just padded around the suite, with its wrap-around views of Shanghai, in the fluffiest white robe I'd ever encountered.

An hour before we were due to meet, I changed into Yúzé's requested outfit: the secretary look. It's amazing that, no matter where you go in the world, men's role-play fantasies vary very little. I'd brought a white silk shirt, which was cropped under my boobs – since Shuyi had told me that Yúzé was a titty man – and a lycra skirt that clung to my butt like its life depended on it. I matched that with black stockings and kitten heels. There was only a two-floor lift ride to Yúzé's penthouse, but I was terrified of running into someone when I was bursting out of every seam. Thankfully, I went undetected and knocked at Yúzé's door.

I've got to admit, I was pleasantly surprised. Yúzé was nice to look at and nice in nature too – considering that flying a girl halfway around the world just for two hours *had* to be a power move. If anything, he looked even younger than twenty, and despite his wealth he was wearing a suit that seemed too big for him. We couldn't really communicate beyond smiles and gestures, but he did greet me in English and ask me my star sign. Bit late if we weren't compatible.

I wasn't watching the clock, but I'd be surprised if the sex lasted more than ten minutes. He was easy to please: some oral, some boobs pushed in his face, condom on and then missionary. He was super chill afterwards – like, that was all he came for and now he'd get going, thanks. *Ker-ching* – I was $20,000 richer.

Not long after I got back to my room, Shuyi rang and asked if I'd like to join her for dinner in one of the hotel restaurants. It necessitated another outfit change – this time to a long-sleeved, knee-length dress – but I was ravenous, now that she mentioned it. When I met her on the mezzanine, I put her in her mid-thirties, dressed elegantly but chastely, as though trying to overcompensate for whatever I might turn up in. Don't draw any attention to the boss and all that.

Shuyi helped me navigate the menu, which – even though it was translated to English – was still a mystery to me. The sashimi platter included raw horse meat, and Shuyi ordered small dishes of sea anemone and jellyfish. I felt like Julia Roberts in *Pretty Woman* trying to eat snails: 'Slippery little suckers!'

Halfway through, after some stilted conversation, Shuyi pulled the rug and revealed that she'd done some escorting in the past, which instantly got me interested. Sex work sounded like another level of hectic in China, and her dates absolutely had to look like that: just dates. I guess she had a VPN, because she was very familiar with my profile and had lots of questions about how I ran my business in Australia.

With Shuyi's help, I managed to negotiate more money from Yúzé so that I could upgrade to business on the way home. I know, I know; I bigged up my ability to fly economy earlier. But having made the Singapore and Shanghai trips back to back, I was suddenly clobbered by exhaustion. As Shuyi predicted, Yúzé didn't blink an eye and immediately transferred the money. I guess he had a good time.

Now that my profile has grown even bigger, I wouldn't risk a visit to Shanghai again – I would not survive in a Chinese prison. Things ran unbelievably smoothly on that trip, but I'm a firm believer in not pushing your luck.

From Miami to the Hollywood Hills

Steeple your fingers together. That's the average size of the piles of cocaine circulating on the yacht I boarded with Eden one morning in Miami. We left Island Gardens Marina and anchored on an island called Elliott Key, and pretty soon I had no concept of what time it was anymore.

'Bend over!' the bronzed, buff guy urged me for the second time, playfully slapping my ass. I gave a regulation giggle and obliged, wriggling my butt as I leaned forwards. I felt the long side of his American Express card dancing across my skin. They love the big butts in Miami. The guy and three unknown participants, who would have looked exactly like him, took turns snorting long lines of party powder from my golden globes. 'Incredible,' the guy said, giving my ass another slap.

Yacht girls and cocaine – they're a must for any millionaire playboy's party. From Cannes to Cancun, yachting is a rite of passage for a model-slash-sex-worker. The subtext is you're paid to party, with 'partying' including opening your legs. I barely had a conversation with the guy who invited me and Eden. He may have been a rapper. He looked like a rapper. He just rounded up a bunch of guys, a bunch of girls, and was intent on throwing the ultimate party; he probably did so every week. Maybe some girls were booked through an agency, but Eden and I were flying solo. Ever since we'd arrived in Miami people had been inviting us to yacht parties and VIP booths at clubs. It seemed like anything went in Miami, if you were game.

One night, Eden and I were in a club called Exotica when we spotted one of our favourite content creators, the Flesh Mechanic. He was known for his big sexy mo and his irreverent attitude, and we were totally obsessed with him, so we downed a shot and approached him. Our opener was 'Do you want to fuck in the bathrooms?' He did. We had a messy threesome in a stall before a bouncer banged on the door and kicked us out of the club. We never did get to know Señor Flesh properly, but he's forever emblazoned in our hearts.

It wasn't always cool, though. Men in Miami can be super-aggressive in the way they approach you. One guy pulled his car up next to us on the street and invited us to a yacht party, which we politely declined. He then followed us for blocks, screaming abuse. This was broad daylight in the city, but no one came to help. We had to keep walking past our hotel so that he wouldn't know where we were staying, and eventually he got bored and drove off.

In the case of the cocaine cruise, the maybe-rapper's friend approached us at a club and we talked a while, then he just told us to be at the marina at 11am if we wanted to party. We did. I'd watched plenty of Girls Gone Wild videos in my time – the porn franchise where girls get drunk and naked on boats and by the pool. Girls competing to be the wildest? I like a challenge.

This party did not disappoint. By the time we reached Elliott Key, we were all topless and soaked from champagne showers. If you have to ask, a champagne shower entails girls being doused by the contents of a bottle of Brignac. Money was nothing. The cocaine was flowing just as freely, and groups of people frequently retired below deck to fuck, or didn't bother with privacy and did it right out in the open. Sometimes horny men on other yachts literally jumped overboard to swim over and try to join in. They were helped back into the water by some spirited kicks from the guys on our boat. You couldn't blame them for trying. You could probably hear the booty-clapping as far as Barbados.

I can't say I made any lasting connections that day. Everyone there was there with a purpose – to get paid and/or to get high – and they'd likely never see each other again. The conversation was superficial. I noticed many girls were on something even before we set sail, which I guess is natural when you've got to break the ice fast and be the life of the party. We don't really do that in Australia, so it freaked me out a bit. I did down a lot of champagne, but I'd never want to be in a vulnerable position or unable to charm my way out of a scrape.

That same trip, in Los Angeles, Eden and I were in a bar with a local creator when we were approached by some guys who ran an OnlyFans agency. Drew and Cam brought over a bottle of champagne. They definitely sat at the smarmy end of the charm spectrum and I felt my guard go up immediately. I'd heard about these kinds of agencies. For a mere 50 per cent (minimum) of all your earnings, they offer to book you fancy shoots and collabs, and provide you with cheap-ass marketing and 'chatters' (offshore workers who pretend to be you, sexting your subscribers). They make huge promises to make you a star, but always underdeliver. At best, the approach is one-size-fits-all; at worst it's a total scam. If you hand over all control to your channel, you run the risk of them stealing your content and/or saying generic, inauthentic shit to your subscribers that will scare off your fanbase.

Still, a free meal is a free meal, so we joined them and some other creators at an upscale steakhouse nearby. I recognised a couple of the girls, because they had massive profiles and I'd spent some time in my baby-creator days trying to figure out all their tricks. These agencies dangle big-name creators in front of you so that you assume that your own big moment in the sun will be next.

Drew and Cam went all-out, ordering giant T-bone steaks at $200 a pop. The drill was that we could order whatever we wanted all night – food, drink, drugs – and Eden and I took that brief very seriously. It seemed that this agency was buying girls dinner here practically every night and I guess that's where most of their marketing budget went, because everything else was just smoke and mirrors. The party they invited us to later, for example: it was in one of the mega-mansions in the Calabasa area, but I could tell everything was on hire for the night and that this was just another form of recruitment drive. In California there are private jets you can book by the hour for photo shoots – without the plane ever taking off – to give the illusion of extreme wealth, and while Cam and Drew were ostentatiously sporting Cartier watches on their wrists, I knew you could get them on hire for a few hundred bucks a month. I hate that kind of artifice, where people fake wealth to make wealth. In reality, it's like some fucked-up pyramid scheme where everyone likely loses.

Eden and I are really suss on men of this type, but the other girls were in awe. When our Ubers pulled up at the mansion, the girls took full advantage of the moment to film each other turning in slow circles of wonder next to the big fountain outside. Inside, it was wall-to-wall content creators blinding each other with their light attachments. There was the odd C-list celebrity and NBA player in the mix, evident because they were the only ones not filming themselves.

I guess Drew and Cam thought Eden and I were still considering our options, because a few days later they got in touch again, this time inviting us to a party in the Hills at the house of a singer from an eighties metal band. Of *course* we were going to go to that, for shits and giggles. The party was held in what looked to me, in my wasted state, like a medieval castle. The massive foyer was lit by torches on the wall, and we had to stumble up what felt like a thousand steps in the near-dark. I needed an oxygen tank by the time I was halfway up that staircase. No wonder the singer looked like a semi-revived corpse.

Inside the main room, things were *not* rock'n'roll. The music was at a polite volume and people were desperately mugging the passing waiters carrying trays of canapes so that they could plug their mouths with shrimp and avoid talking to each other.

Eden and I colluded in the corner for a bit, playing a quick round of fuck, marry, kill. Then they started playing 'Señorita' by Shawn Mendes and Camila Cabello, and I broke out the cha-cha-cha. I couldn't help it – after a few drinks my brain wants to go straight back to my Zumba class days. Honestly, it didn't improve the overall vibe, but this time I wasn't getting paid to lift anyone else's mood, so they were on their own.

Sex Tips from Sex Workers

My sex worker friends are hands-down the loveliest, most caring, genuine people I've ever met. Not only am I surrounded by sex-positive souls who have seen every imaginable facet of the human experience up close, but they've been happy to share all their insider knowledge.

In the spirit of better sex and better sexual health, I'm happy to pass on what I've learned. I want all of us to thrive in our sexuality.

How to taste good

If you find certain foods linger through your sweat glands and skin, you can guarantee they'll affect the way you taste, too. Coffee, spices, garlic, onion, the flavours in junk food – even red meat, fatty foods and alcohol can give you a sour taste. (Okay, I know you've probably seen me make a blue cheese martini for the clout on TikTok but, trust me, I wouldn't drink that just before seeing a client.) Adult performers of all genders improve the taste of their cum by drinking pineapple juice and other particularly sweet fruits such as kiwi, berries and papaya. Hydration also helps: think about how your pee is darker and more pungent if you're dehydrated. It's the same for your pussy juices.

If none of that's working and there's a lingering smell, it could be bacterial vaginosis (BV), which is basically an unhappy microbiome. If your vaginal bacteria is off-balance you can get a greyish discharge and a really ponging fishy smell. It's easily treated by a pessary from the pharmacy, but many people take a while to cotton on to having it. If they've never heard of BV they might catch a whiff and assume they need to keep scrubbing themselves clean, but ironically, soap can really throw off your vagina's pH and exacerbate the condition further – which is why it's always best to use a gynaecologist-approved, pH-balanced intimate wash. If the BV has really taken hold, you might need a course of antibiotics to clear it ... and antibiotics can give you thrush. Sigh. I didn't even know myself before I got it checked out at the clinic; I thought I must have mistakenly left a period sponge wedged up there and I was getting flashbacks to the whole 'toxic shock' panic at high school.

If you find you keep getting BV, the source might be your sexual partner, because the offending bacteria can be harboured on the penis – in fact, in 2025, BV started to be categorised as an STI. So the only real way to prevent reinfection is for the guy to take antibiotics (which means persuading him that he's the problem even though he himself doesn't have any symptoms. Good luck, girlies; show him this book if it helps).

How to ask a guy to clean his goddamn penis

Now for the elephant in the room: what if a guy's cock smells bad? Sometimes it's down to a tight foreskin under which the smeg (gag) can build up, sometimes it's down to poor hygiene. Either way, bringing it up is awkward as fuck if you're not a sex worker. In an ideal world you'd be as direct as me, but I get that matters can be more delicate if it's someone you're romantically interested in. Almost every 'civilian' woman I've polled has admitted to putting on a cringeworthy cutesy voice to try and seem less demanding, or to just putting up with it.

I recommend a line like this: 'I really want to go to town on you. Why don't you take a shower and join me in the bedroom?' That only works if it's before he's undressed, though, otherwise it's obvious you just caught a whiff.

If it's too late and you're at the jocks-off stage, you could suggest that the pair of you take a shower *together* ('Let's get naked in the shower'). He won't know whether you're worried about your own smell or gagging at his. Or, for god's sake, just gently tell him. The things we do to preserve the male ego ...

How to give a good blowjob

First off, every man likes different things, so it's best to ask for feedback; but there are some techniques to try:

- **Make eye contact.** If the angle makes that difficult, you can occasionally pull his cock out of your mouth and tilt your head up at him as you rub it or slap it on your face.
- **Gag theatrically.** Few men aren't thrilled by the idea that their cock is so big it's making you choke.
- **Relax your throat.** While not every girl enjoys giving deep throat, even just letting the tip of his cock bump the back of your throat gives him a whole 'nother sensation.
- **Use your tongue.** Softly lick the tip of his cock and the extra-sensitive

part at the back of the head, technically known as the frenulum.

- **Don't neglect his balls.** Some guys love to have their whole sack sucked, while for others the most sensitive part of their genitalia is where the bottom of the shaft meets their balls.

- **Wetter is better:** Use lots of spit and don't be afraid to trail it from your mouth to his cock for a hot visual. Word of warning, though: don't attempt a full-blown *hawk-tuah* if you have a cold, as yellow isn't a good look.

- **Avoid scraping with your teeth.** But experiment with very gently dragging your nails on his shaft.

- **Try adding your hands.** Some guys like you to work the shaft vigorously with your hand while sucking the head, given that he'd be jerking off much the same way. Others like the more subtle approach of stroking his cock and gently twisting your hand all the way up over the tip, alternating between that and sucking.

- **Utilise a toy.** You can experiment with how much he's game for by running the tip of a vibrator on the base of his cock, his balls, his perineum (also known as his taint) and his asshole. He'll definitely let you know. See also anilingus.

How to squirt

Can all women squirt? No. But I guarantee that more women can squirt than currently realise they can. There are definitely porn performers who fake it, and there are others who just try to pee and see what happens.

The most accepted explanation of squirting is that it's a high-velocity mix of pee and female ejaculation from the Skene's glands, which are either side of the urethra. (These glands were named by a male gynaecologist in 1880. I can only hope Alexander Skene made his wife a very happy woman.) Make sure you drink lots of water beforehand, so that if you do pee it's clear in colour and doesn't smell. I drink two litres of water and an electrolyte drink to replenish my levels of sodium and potassium, the same way you would after a hard workout.

A waterfall is my favourite thing to do with a client. It may sound like a golden shower, but actually it's squirting, or gushing, on a guy. One client used to love me gushing on his face, which I also loved because it was an extra $1000.

For me, in the early days, it was a mental game. I was so in my head about wanting to do it with another person that there was often too much pressure. I started practising in private, so that I could really let go. Now, on a good day, I can hit the ceiling. Vibration is key, so you could try a toy up your pussy, pressing against your g-spot, as well as stimulating your clit.

Fucking while on your period

Sex workers take bookings while having their periods. Their secret weapon is the menstrual sponge, which is pushed up past the pelvic floor muscle, and is soft enough to be undetected by the client. You can buy these from sex shops, either online or on the high street. It's possible that on your heaviest flow day you might get some leakage, but day three onwards always works well for me. The drawback is that, unlike with a tampon, there's no string, so occasionally I've had to enlist Jackson to help me get it out. The official advice is to try removing it in the bath or shower, because when it's wet (and when you're relaxed) it's easier to remove, or to squat – the action of which pushes the sponge down. Use a sponge once and destroy.

One thing to consider when having sex during your period is to be extra hygienic, using an intimate wash regularly, especially just before sex. If you have your period, bacteria can build up if you use the same pad or tampon for too long, and pads can be particularly smelly because the blood reacts with oxygen in the air. Using a silicone cup instead can help.

How to enjoy anal

It can be entirely enjoyable to have your butt railed on a whim, without any preparation, but for anyone who's considering a long, hard session, I do have some prep advice.

Some women like to 'warm themselves up' by stretching their ring with a butt plug, which can be worn discreetly all day, or they might spend an intensive thirty minutes with a training toy. The risk of not warming up first is that the anal tissue is more delicate than vaginal, and can result in a tear if the fucking is too vigorous. My own training kit, developed in collaboration with Vush, has three butt plugs that progress in size, with a T-bar handle for easy insertion and removal. It's basically what I wish I could have bought when I first started having anal.

Over time, having regular anal develops a kind of muscle memory, but I'd recommend always using lube for both warm-ups and the deed itself.

Lastly, never go from anal to vaginal without the guy cleaning his cock first. The bacteria can play havoc with your pussy's ecosystem.

How to have anal without worrying about mess

Like the 2023 TikTok trend told us, hot girls have stomach issues. So many girlies have IBS and/or hormone-related digestive distress, so the thought of anal sex frankly makes us shit ourselves. What if things get messy?

Ideally, an anal-loving guy would realise that such sex comes with risks and it wouldn't bother him a bit; but even if that's the case, the person on the receiving end can feel self-conscious. The good news is there are ways around it. The bad news is it's a bit of a chore. The reason I charge $15,000 for anal – apart from to put people off, since it's not my favourite thing – is the prep takes twice as long as the booking, and it interrupts my natural flow for a few days.

Step one is to figure out your 'transit time'. My anal idol, Angela White, uses that expression to describe the length of time it takes for your average meal to travel through your body, leaving you 'clean' – and it's different for every person. You can figure it out by having a meal with corn, since corn isn't properly digested and is visible in the toilet bowl. For Angela the transit time is about twelve hours, so before she's due to film an anal scene she fasts for at least twelve hours. She'll eat something nutritious, such as nut butter or a protein bar, just before starting the scene.

Step two is to douche. If you're not shooting porn you certainly don't need a full-blown enema – unless you enjoy that sort of thing. Just buy a silicone douche from the pharmacy. You fill it with warm water and squirt it up your butt, expelling the liquid over the toilet bowl. Don't have sex for about an hour, because there may still be some residue.

In terms of general maintenance, I use soluble fibre supplements every day to stay regular, and if I know I'm going to have anal I'll also take Gastro-Stop as a safety net.

After everything I've put it through, my backdoor deserves to be treated like a princess.

Paypiggies and Findom

Have you ever seen a wishlist linked on a beautiful girl's social media profile? And then wondered about the suckers who are supposedly gifting her home decor, Cartier jewellery, lip fillers and mortgage repayments? Does it sound too good to be true? It absolutely is – most of the time.

There's a tendency among these princesses, as they're sometimes called, to exaggerate how many gifts they're getting. Don't get me wrong – there are some professional financial doms who are damn good at what they do – but for the most part I think these girls are just putting their desire out to the universe in the hope that it will provide: in the form of a man with more money than sense.

This is the world of financial domination (findom). Men are the finsubs – or paypigs – who are bullied into handing over their earnings, and who get off on that bullying. The women might be fierce doms who shit-talk the sub; or pampered princesses who need to be cared for; or regal queens; or goddesses who need to be worshipped. As such, these women need to be damn good at role-play, because there are no sexual favours in this equation. They're like a sugar daddy, but without the sugar.

I hate to be the bearer of bad news, but it's really hard to get a guy to give you all his money without you putting out. You can take it from me that it also costs a woman a LOT to look luxurious and high-maintenance enough to attract these men in the first place. If she isn't wealthy, she's got to really make it *look* that way, posting pictures of yachts and designer cars – either posing in front of someone else's or just finding the pictures online. Sometimes she'll post screenshots of cash apps with money coming in, but she'll have doctored those. These guys don't go for broke girls – they're into the chase, and want to feel that they are found worthy by a woman who is dripping with class and money.

After all that, the man who is into financial domination is practically a unicorn. I've managed to bag a few, but before long they gallop off to the next pretty girl and I'm left clutching my receipts, resigned to returning my latest haul to the shop so that I can at least cash my chips.

A word of safety advice for anyone dipping a toe into findom: avoid Amazon wishlists. If you fill your cart and allow a man to buy, anything that's sold by third-party sellers will reveal your name and address to him. Also, he might order your goodies, send you the proof and then cancel the order – but now he has your address. There are other sites that are specifically set up for wishlists that keep your details safe. It's important to do your research.

~

While I've never specialised in findom, I do have some very generous clients. Guys have taken me on a lot of shopping trips, basically giving me their credit card and watching me buy designer clothes. Others have given me their credit card and asked me to video myself in the clothes later. My longest trot was with a CEO in Sydney: dark hair, quite attractive, dressed smart-casual – a nice shirt tucked into designer jeans. He'd already paid for me to stay in a luxurious penthouse suite at the Hilton, and then we went shopping in King Street and Castlereagh Street, where all the fancy shops are. He said I had $20,000 to spend. I might have looked like his daughter, but I think a lot of the retail staff caught on because of the tight-fitting clothes I was trying on.

Another guy sent me thousands of dollars to spend on a trip to Europe I was really excited about. I bought a bunch of dresses and lots of gizmos to make the long-haul flight more tolerable. I made sure to only send him videos of me modelling the top-of-the-range neck cushions, not the matching ones I'd bought for Jackson and the kids. Another time, a regular client gifted me a one-off chunk of money and I bought items to make care packages for a local domestic violence shelter – a cause close to my heart after my experience in my teens. That might not have been what he intended me to spend his wages on, but he did say it was up to me.

These are often guys with salaries really deep into the six figures, and they love to relinquish their control and be bossed around. You have to read what they want pretty quickly: a girl who's bratty and demanding? Or someone who's downright nasty? The trick is not to hesitate, to leave no room for doubt. If they want a brat, I channel Cher from *Clueless*. I ask them what they're even doing messaging me and tell them they're wasting my precious time. They should be emptying their bank account because I deserve better. If they dare to ask for a picture, I send a photo of my rubbish bin.

If I can tell they want me a few notches meaner, I channel the bitch nurse from the eating disorder ward, only instead of making them feel bad about their bodies I'll roast their designer watch or their choice of sunglasses. I'll tell them I know they can't stop fantasising about my ass and that's all they're good for, unless they can prove otherwise.

Honestly, I find it easier and easier to talk down to men the longer I stay in this job.

One girl I know said she found findom to be really therapeutic, having come out of a controlling relationship. It felt good to have the boot on the other foot, but with nobody coming to any harm. Personally, I do always keep an eye on a guy who might be spending beyond his means.

Case in point: Rodney. He was nineteen years old, fresh over from South Africa, and he would book me constantly when I was on tour in Sydney. Rodney was skinny, petite, nervy-looking. The poor guy had no confidence. He was really sweet but I'd have to work so hard to get a conversation going.

Rodney was lonely. There are some guys who are so isolated, they just crave some company and to actually be *seen*. I felt bad for him because he didn't have any community in Australia and barely any social life or skills. It was so easy to take money off him. When our time was up, I might say, 'You can book another hour if you want,' and immediately he would extend the session by another $1500. It always surprised me, because I'd think, *Are you actually enjoying yourself?* A session would consist of a little bit of sex and then me basically sitting there talking to myself – and yet, I'd wind up turning down other clients because Rodney kept on extending and extending.

Eventually, on one tour, I asked how he could afford to see me so much. I knew he was at university and didn't have a job. Was he royalty or something? It turned out he had been hit by a car and had received a massive payout. Maybe because he had no social life to splash money on – as many young men would – he was spending it on me. He must have dropped $50,000 within five weeks of knowing me. Now that I knew he didn't have a pipeline of funds from Daddy, I gave him a financial lecture. I remember it so vividly. We'd had sex and were lounging on the bed facing each other. Remembering all the people who'd been kind enough to give me financial advice over the previous few years, I sat up and got serious.

'Rodney, you need to get your shit together and stop wasting your money,' I said. 'Enjoy yourself every now and then, sure, but you should be investing. Read up on the markets. Buy some crypto. You *have* to start saving for the future!'

Rodney tore his eyes from my tits, which were bouncing a bit from my emphatic points.

'Really?'

For the next twenty minutes I talked him through the property market and the sorts of questions he should be asking an accountant. He took it on board – or, at least, I never saw him again. Maybe he just moved along to the next Gold Coast queen. I do like to get mama bear on a young guy when necessary, though. I'm happy to fulfil their fantasies for a handsome price, but if they're a nice person I don't want to suck them dry.

You Want Me to Send You WHAT?

I remember the first time I farted in front of a boyfriend. I wanted to die. Ordinarily, if I felt one building to a peak, I'd make my excuses, go to the bathroom and put the cold tap on full blast to mask any ricocheting sound. As for taking a dump within a 50 mile radius of a guy – I would literally have to be months into a relationship before allowing him to entertain the idea that I, too, had bodily functions.

That was then, this is now.

Now, I catch my farts in jars like butterflies and send them to collectors. Don't pretend you wouldn't, too. Seriously, if it's got to come out anyway, why not capture it and make a heap of money? (Even more money if the client requests that you video yourself executing it.) Why is it only guys that can find farts funny? Why can't I enjoy catching mine, covering the jar in cute stickers and making a TikTok video about it? Shame is like a spark: it only spreads if you fan it. Talking of which, I wonder if my farts would catch fire if the guy was smoking when he opened the jar? I'd ask him to try but he probably wouldn't want to waste it. He's so into gassy ladies that he knows to recommend me beans, lentils and Metamucil fibre powder to make the process more efficient.

By the time my fart goes off into the world, in its little jar with a pink bow and a handwritten note with hearts dotting the i's, I feel pretty good about myself, and a whole lot lighter. I might even turn my farts into a signature scent. I'd call it Shameless.

Think of anything gross and I guarantee you there's a market for it: used tampons and panty liners (one client wanted my period sponge after we'd finished having sex); jars of pee (sometimes I'll get a return video of a guy chugging it, but as soon as I realise what I'm watching, it gets deleted); toenail clippings; pubic hair clippings; vials of spit. Don't yuck someone's yum, as the kink-conservationists say.

There are so many imaginative kinks that started in Japan that OnlyFans creators have enthusiastically leapt upon. Burusera is the fetish for used underwear, and got so big in the nineties that you could find vending machines full of them. Troublingly, they tended to make the claim that they were schoolgirls' underwear; on a more positive note, I know plenty of grown-ass OnlyFans women who make a great buck wearing a cheap pair of panties all day and mailing it off. Used socks have their own fan club, too.

Oshouji is the practice of using calligraphy to write erotic words on a woman's body. When creators do it, it tends to be clumsily lettered obscenities and arrows pointing to various body parts. That's not to be confused with osouji, which is a big cleaning ritual the Japanese do at New Year. I can't imagine a situation where that confusion would get you in trouble, but you never know.

By far the grossest thing I've been asked for is my BV discharge. As I mentioned in the chapter Sex Tips From Sex Workers, BV stands for bacterial vaginosis, and it's easily treated by a pessary from the pharmacy once you've been checked out by a doctor. I put that off for a few days because of this special request. The client loved BV precisely for its very pungent smell, so when I made a TikTok video moaning about my stank he immediately messaged me and asked that I send him a sample. I cannot emphasise enough how bad I had made this smell sound in the video. I believe my exact words were: 'It's like something has crawled up there and died. I've been cleaning my kitchen, trying to see if some mystery meat has rolled under the fridge or if one of my cats has surprised me with a rotting gift from outside.' So that is what he ordered – at great expense. He bought multiple pairs of my dirty underwear that I'd worn all day. I even used a spoon to scoop some out and smear it on the gusset, in case they didn't look gungy enough. As he's not from Australia, he had to pay a crazy amount of shipping as well. I double vacuum-sealed them so hopefully they got past the sniffer dogs at customs.

Men never cease to amaze me.

We Are Not Dating

When a client orders repeat bookings and I quite enjoy their company, there's a danger that a boundary can become blurred. On the one hand, a sex worker desperately wants to just stick to the cool clients so that she doesn't have to take on any unknown loose cannons. On the other hand, a guy doesn't necessarily have to be lonely to become obsessed with a sex worker. All she has to do is dazzle him with her attention and pretend to be fascinated and even the most successful and seemingly well-adjusted man could start believing there's a really deep connection.

Men don't so much want to rescue me – since I'm clearly doing okay for myself – but they do often hint that they'd be prepared to have me as a girlfriend if I just gave everything up. Yes, that's right: if I just gave up the fancy car, the gifts, the trips overseas, the luxe lifestyle and the dream of buying my two children a house each, they would consider dating me. That might sound naively sweet, but I promise you there's a darker side: it comes with the solid belief that sex workers are total horn-dogs who would fuck anything that moves. From the moment they start hinting that they'd consider it, they're already adding 'jokey' comments like, 'You'd have to leave my friends alone' or 'I wouldn't want to share you, of course.'

Other men with big fat wallets want to sweep me off my feet so that they can enjoy a no-ties prolonged 'girlfriend experience'. I've been invited on holiday to Bali, the Maldives and Hawaii (with one guy apologetically offering Hamilton Island), and I've got to admit I even considered agreeing to the Maldives, but then I had a dream that I got kidnapped, which I took as a sign. We'll see. Maybe one day, if Baby Daddy can come too.

The overnighter girlfriend experience is pretty popular. We'll snuggle up, Netflix and chill, and of course have sex – though I'm always angling to spend as long as possible in my leopard-print onesie. Sometimes it's with guys who have trouble landing a real girlfriend, but often it's someone who has come out of a long-term relationship and isn't ready to go back on the dating scene. Other times, a guy will book me just to play his date out in public for the evening, like at a work event or to go to a sports game. I can read straight away if he wants to have fun shocking people or if he wants me to play it straight ... and at $8000 for an evening with no sex, either is fine by me.

By far the weirdest girlfriend experience I've been embroiled in is when a regular client asked if I would join him for dinner. Jon was a pleasant guy in his late forties who always treated me with a lot of respect. He was clean-cut except for some slightly eccentric sideburns and a soul patch, enjoyed a round of golf and had been divorced for a couple of years. The only strike he had against him was that, after a few months of us meeting up every few weeks for very vanilla sex, he started bringing along terrible PVC costumes that he was obviously ordering online from stripper stores, and asking me to call him 'sir'. They were garishly coloured butt-skimming uncomfortable things that made me cringe and were always too small. But still, there was that very vanilla, very easy sex.

About six months into our faux-lationship, Jon asked, quite coyly, if I would join him for dinner next time. He wanted to take me to a restaurant on the harbour for a good feed, he said. Calculating it would take a couple of hours, I quoted him $4000 and he paid the full amount right there and then.

The day came around and it was time to get ready. It being Jon, I opted for a look that was jusssst about acceptable in public but that would still tick his boxes of being hideous and hard to walk in: red high heels, a black peasant top and a red leather skirt I could barely squeeze my BBL into. I shaved my legs and cooch, just in case Jon got a mind to extend the booking and take us to a hotel, which I thought he probably would with a little persuasion.

The restaurant was a pretty average surf-and-turf joint, and when I walked in I felt a lot of eyes on me. It was popular with families and old couples, it seemed. Frowning, I scanned the room for a lone man. Then I spotted him. Jon was standing up at his table, waving. 'Kayla Jade.' He was using my full name because he'd never got the hang of the fact that my first name is just Kayla. At least he wasn't calling 'Blue Eyed Kayla Jade', I guess.

Sat at Jon's table were three other people. I wasn't wearing my glasses, so they came into focus as I approached on my ridiculously high heels. A woman of about seventy, a teenage girl of about eighteen and a boy of about fourteen. My heart sank. Surely, surely, surely Jon wasn't introducing me to his family?

'This is Kayla Jade,' Jon beamed as I approached, like he was the city mayor presenting an award.

'Hi guys,' I said, in my sweetest voice. I gave them a little wave.

Only the woman smiled back. 'Hello, dear.'

'This is my mother,' Jon said needlessly. 'Mary.'

'I'm so pleased to meet you, Mary,' I said, leaning in for an awkward hug. I had to get a read on this situation fast. Was I going to have to pretend to be Jon's new girlfriend, or was I literally the sex worker he'd been banging every other Sunday? Ahhh, every *other* Sunday, it now dawned on me. That was obviously when he *didn't* have the kids.

'There's a soup special tonight,' Jon said. 'Seafood chowder.'

I made an impressed noise and gratefully hid behind the giant menu that his son passed over. I couldn't help noticing his son was gawking at me.

'This is Lachie,' Jon said, 'and this is Sarah.'

'Hi Sarah,' I said, instinctively greeting the girl first. She looked like she'd take a while to thaw.

'Hi,' she said shortly, tossing back her hair extensions. Bad sign.

'And how old are you, Lachie?' I said, turning my attention to the boy.

'Fourteen,' he said, a slightly despondent note to his voice. Way to go, Kayla, asking a young boy, who's trying to impress, exactly how old he is.

'Wow.'

He studied his menu.

'And what is it you do for work, Kayla Jade?' Mary asked. I panicked, looking at Jon. What the hell had he told them about me?

'Kayla Jade is one of my best students,' Jon said smoothly. My panic eased half a notch. I did remember that Jon was an academic, but I had no idea what the subject was. Something boring. Conveyancing? Town planning? Tax? Also, in what world does a supervisor take his student out for dinner with his family? I waited for more prompts but none came.

'I feel like I really learned a lot under Jon,' I eventually said, and I saw Jon give a slight smirk. Yeah, you wish, buddy.

'Wonderful,' Mary beamed, seemingly satisfied with that.

A waiter came over and took our order. I saw her eyes slide over my cleavage and down to my skirt, which seemed to gleam ruby red under the lights. Discreetly, I took a napkin and spread it over my lap.

'Lovely view,' I said, nodding out to the harbour. Jon and Mary agreed heartily. I could see where he got his manners from – though I wasn't about to let him off the hook for tonight. Maybe I could have some fun, too. 'What was Jon like as a kid?' I asked Mary.

'Oh!' she laughed. 'He was trouble.'

'Really?' I watched Jon squirm. 'I can't imagine that.'

'Oh, yes. He was always messing around with the girls, he was terrible.'

'Gran,' Sarah said, screwing up her face.

I took a big slug of wine. 'Are you still at school, Sarah?'

'Sarah's on a gap year,' Jon said. 'She's going to apply for uni next year, aren't you, darling?'

'I don't know,' she muttered. I felt some sympathy there. I'd never been pushed into further education by my parents and I'd never regretted it.

'Beautiful nails,' I said, gesturing at her talons. She had quite a few rhinestones going on.

'Thanks. I'm going to be a nail technician,' she said. I saw Jon wince.

'Where'd you get them? Paintbox?'

She nodded. 'Yeah. I usually go polygel but I've gone acrylics this time.'

'Good choice.'

Jon looked baffled by our conversation, but I congratulated myself on at least warming up his daughter some. Two wait staff came over with our starters, providing a blessed few minutes of silence as we pointed out who was getting what and settled in with our dishes.

As I sliced into my steak, I tried to catch Jon's eye. Was his kink being brazen? If so, he was sliding way down in my estimation. It's one thing to want to have sex in public where there's a risk of being caught (although, having actually been caught once, by a pool cleaner, I decided never again) but another to mess with your family. Or maybe he was just that special kind of guy, as many academically minded people were, who was genuinely clueless when it came to social etiquette and not hurting other people's feelings.

I caught Lachie staring at me again and I gave him a smile. He snapped his eyes back down to his pasta. Lachie was onto me.

'Did you grow up here, Mary?' I asked.

'God, no,' she said. 'This was all swamp in my day. I'm from Ascot.'

Ah, that figured – it was one of the poshest suburbs of Brisbane. Those old money families could be pretty weird. We all chewed some more.

'And you?' she eventually asked.

'New Zealand,' I said. 'A little town on the North Island.'

'Oh, wonderful,' she said. 'What's it called?'

I paused. 'Whanganui,' I said, choosing a more picturesque town than Palmy. My tone of voice had implied I came from somewhere adorable and I didn't want to let her down. Although ... why the hell not? I wasn't *actually* Jon's girlfriend, I reminded myself.

'What's your thesis on?' Sarah interrupted. I regarded her and she coolly held my gaze. To my ears, Sarah's newfound interest sounded a bit too innocent. Lachie stared at me again, his open mouth full of food.

I glanced at Jon, who had his own mouth full. Fuck.

'It's pretty complicated,' I said, willing Jon to chew faster. I was so tempted just to blow this mug's cover: *Actually, I have a PhD in cocksmoking.* 'Jon can probably explain it better.'

He raised his eyebrows. Chew, chew. I stared at his bland face and his stupid little soul patch that he probably thought made him look alternative. I suddenly hated him. If he thought I was going to try to sweet-talk him into an extension after this little performance, he was insane. No, sir.

'What were you saying about my ideas the other day, Jon?'

'I said you were legally compliant,' he said, having a little chuckle to himself.

I sighed, mentally adding another $2000 to Jon's tally. He'd probably pay it. It was basically danger money, for everything he was putting me through. Fuck him, I thought.

'Jon is very popular with his students,' I offered, wondering what he'd do with that.

'Yeah, we know,' Sarah said, checking her lipstick. 'But they don't last long.'

Jon had another little chuckle.

'That's enough, dear,' Mary said, although which of them she was addressing, I had no idea anymore.

The wait staff took away our plates. I should have known no client could ever be as easy as Jon had seemed to be. There was always a goddamn catch.

'I'm just going to the bathroom,' I said cheerfully. After a split second's hesitation, I took my shoulder bag with me. Any pretence that I was actually coming back was an insult to us all.

'Bye, Kayla Jade,' Lachie said sadly. God help that kid.

It was still light as I waited for my Uber outside. I swear I will never understand men. Did Jon's mother know his game all along? Did she know my game? Later that night, Jon sent a few weird texts – 'Are you okay? Did you have a good night? Did you enjoy your meal??' – but I ghosted him.

Sorry, Jon. It's not me, it's you.

The Client Who Broke My Heart

I once went on a podcast – probably when I had full-blown premenstrual dysphoric disorder – and stone-faced told the interviewer that I felt *nothing* for my clients. I think she was a bit shocked. But it's part of my job description to make a guy believe that we have an incredible connection, when the reality is I'll forget him the moment the door closes. For many men, if they get to bathe in the glow of a woman's full attention, they mistake that for something super-profound, without even considering whether they've given that woman something back to warrant it.

So I know it can sometimes sound like I'm jaded and that I have no empathy towards clients, but that's not always the case. Sometimes I do get a little bit attached.

There are some very cool reasons that people see sex workers. Maybe they've come out of a long-term relationship, but they can't face the thought of dating and don't want to lead a girl on. Maybe they want to try something specific that a previous partner had never been into.

Maybe their life feels stagnant and they want to treat themselves with a bit of adventure. Maybe their sex drive is higher than/different to their partner's and they have permission to explore. You can tell when someone has never seen a sex worker before. I mean, usually they want to *tell* me it's their first time, but also, they're usually shaking, which I find really cute.

One of my very favourite, sweetest clients was a guy in his mid-seventies who always brought me flowers from his garden. I couldn't get over seeing him dressed in his Sunday best, clutching his favourite blooms. He loved gardening and gave me advice on how to tackle the bugs plaguing my lemon trees. When he first messaged me I was a bit worried because he sounded so sweet. I wrote back: 'Do you know what I actually do? Do you want company?' He replied that he'd always loved curves on a woman. I was impressed he even knew how to get in touch with me – did he have a grandkid showing him, or is gramps just really in touch with the times? And I don't know if he took Viagra, but he actually had more stamina than most guys half his age. He was tuned in and appreciative.

The first time I saw him he apologised for being old, which broke my heart. I mean, do douchebags apologise for being douchebags? I told him, 'You're seventy-four years young, and thank you for being so considerate.'

Some clients are chatty. They love hearing about my sex work and the collabs and the porn shoots overseas. I don't mind talking about it because I actually love going deep in a one-to-one conversation – it's my ADHD brain. Sometimes they want to talk about their favourite porn stars who got into escorting, and do I know them. It's starry-eyed stuff. Often they will ask me about my own life, and I'll know they're a good guy if they immediately pick up on the fact that my personal life is off-limits.

Another client who really got me in the feels, Jamie, had booked me for two hours. I spent ten minutes stroking his cock and blowing him, but he just couldn't get hard, and he asked me to stop. Now, this guy was in his forties, nice-looking, really lovely and polite. A catch, actually. I couldn't figure out why he had booked me, because his heart didn't seem to be in it, so I straight out asked him. He said his friends had been on at him to get out of the house and do something, throw his hat back in the ring. It turned out his wife had died of cancer a few years before. They'd been so in love and then she got sick. He hadn't been with anyone since and he couldn't imagine the idea of it.

For the rest of the booking, I rubbed Jamie's back as he sat and cried. He told me all about his wife, how artsy she was, how they did everything together. Her illness had been so cruel. Slowly, the cancer robbed her of her mobility and then her cognitive functions. Since her death he would drag himself to work each day, then go home to a house that was empty, but for their cat. Damn, he loved that cat. There was such sadness in his eyes that I found myself crying too.

Some clients don't really need to get off; they just have skin hunger. They need to be touched and shown some intimacy. We all release oxytocin when we bond with someone through skin touch, whether it be the mother nurturing her baby, the person giving their partner a massage, or the friend soothing another by stroking their arm. We can even release it without touch, by eye-gazing, or asking gentle questions. These are all tools at a sex worker's disposal, but we don't always feel that the opportunity presents itself. It's quite special when it does.

I think of Jamie often and I'll always have a tender spot for him. I hope he's okay.

Couples Therapy

If you've ever used ChatGPT to find the right words to fix your relationship with your partner, or just rewrite that pissy text you were about to send them, you're definitely not alone – but maybe you could try a more adventurous approach when you hit a stalemate.

Even though your girl has to work extra hard, I absolutely love seeing couples. Like, it warms my heart. I've never had the sense that one person coerced the other into booking a sex worker; in fact, the best thing about it is that both parties are so excited that you can see their bond strengthen in front of your eyes. I'd estimate that nine times out of ten it's the woman who makes the arrangements. One woman even paid me extra to peg her husband – on her birthday, no less – which I guess made her a female cuck: a cuckquean.

My favourite couple of all time booked me as a radical form of couples therapy. Darren and Carly had been together twenty years, and their youngest kid was soon to leave home. In theory, anyway – house prices these days, hey? When the kids grow up it can trigger a crisis in a couple's relationship. They start to question how happy they are and how complacent they've become and if they really need each other anymore. Sometimes their relationship will implode when one party has an affair, but these two decided to tackle things head on together: first with date nights, then with trying new things.

It was a surprisingly quick journey from pottery classes to seeing a sex worker. In between these two points, Carly and Darren tried MDMA therapy, where they took the drug and cuddled and talked through their relationship with a therapist; and also thirty-six questions – conversation starters designed by social psychologist Arthur Aron to improve intimacy and understanding, leading to love. They didn't want to open up their marriage, but thought that seeing a sex worker together would be an interesting way to explore their desires and find more common ground.

This couple was so cute. They turned up to the pizza restaurant holding hands. They'd dressed up nice: Darren in a pastel linen shirt with a few buttons undone, tucked into jeans, and Carly in a summery midi dress with gold jewellery. They made a good-looking couple, actually. I just had to make sure *they* could see that.

Right from the get-go, the evening was super chill. They'd booked me for hours because they wanted to take their time and treat it like a date, with a period of us getting to know each other. They tried some of those thirty-six questions out on me as I ploughed my way through a seafood pizza: 'If you could wake up tomorrow having gained any one quality or ability, what would it be?' And 'When did you last cry in front of another person?' I can't tell you my answers – you'd fall in love with me and that just makes my job really complicated. What was really nice about this is that they'd obviously decided to make the evening as comfortable for me as I was going to make it for them. It's good when people take initiative like that and remember you're a real person. Also, each person in a couple gets charged for the booking, so it's a double rate. In other words, this investment in their future was costing $16,000. I have to respect that.

After we'd eaten we went for a sunset stroll on the foreshore to walk it off a bit. It was a really pretty evening, and though we must have looked a bit odd – a couple holding hands on a romantic walk, with the woman also arm in arm with me – I didn't care. I was into these vibes.

Up in the hotel suite at the casino, Darren and Carly went off into the shower together and I could hear hushed voices and giggling over the water. They came out in matching robes – cute – suddenly looking a bit shy. I'd stripped down to a baby pink bra, panties and garter set. The golden rule is to always give the woman more attention in these scenarios and make her comfortable, so I invited them both to join me on the bed, but chose Carly to make out with first. I kissed her softly, feeling her respond and lean into me. I love that first moment of kissing a woman, with her pillowy lips and soft skin.

Carly was in her late forties and had told me that she was perimenopausal. She was worried about losing her sex drive, but I think there is often more to it than that. The real problem is likely being taken for granted by your partner, and you, in turn, not being very excited by them anymore. Certainly, she didn't feel hesitant to me right now, as her hand traced down my side and sought out my breasts.

Giving Carly one last deep, tonguing kiss, I turned to Darren and brought his face towards mine. After a brief make-out I suggested that they kiss each other. Darren was rock hard already, so Carly fished his cock out of his robe as they pashed and started stroking it. Quickly they decided to ditch the robes altogether.

I was getting the vibe that Carly might be bisexual, whether she realised it or not, so I asked her if she'd like me to go down on her. Whether she'd want to reciprocate afterwards was the real test. My pussy was douched so clean that you could eat dessert out of it. It's not like I don't make an effort with a male client, but when there's a woman involved too I think we do probably have an unconscious vulva-off – a surreptitious compare and contrast. Carly had a beautiful fleshy cunt that my tongue could get lost in. I could tell how turned on she was by how swollen she was getting.

'Can you cum for me?' I asked her, then finger-fucked her over the edge. She lay back, flushed and laughing.

We spent a leisurely two hours on that bed. Carly was eager to see me suck her husband's cock, then she asked him to fuck her from behind as she went facedown in my pussy. I couldn't tell if she generally called the shots in the relationship, or if Darren was just hanging back in this situation to let her take the lead, but, either way, she was thriving.

They were a loving couple, not into the idea of swinging or a regular throuple. I got that, and I was happy to be their unicorn. The few times I've been to swingers' parties or club nights I've found them to be a pretty average experience – more about being performative than being genuinely hot. In this hotel room, we could relax, ditch the mannered moans and groans, and disintegrate into one big human puddle.

Carly and Darren became semi-regulars for a while, before they were ready to take off the training wheels and go wild on their own. The next time around, Carly brought along a leather harness that fitted over her lingerie, and a whip for Darren to use. They didn't really need me, but by the end of it, I kinda wanted them to adopt me.

Catching Feelings

Mr Sheffield was so named because – as I told him when we were very drunk on our first date – he looked like Mr Sheffield from *The Nanny*. I don't think he was impressed by that comparison, because he paused mid-stroke, but I meant it as a compliment. If you're not familiar with that dope nineties sitcom, Mr Sheffield is a very handsome and tasteful older man. I'd had a crush on him since I was young, and now that I was fucking his doppelganger I couldn't quite believe my luck.

Wait ... did I say 'date'? Yeah, you read that right. The second time we met, I told Mr Sheffield he didn't have to book. Picture us, sickeningly cute, smiling at each other over our coffees in a cafe in the city and suddenly acting shy. A date, in case you haven't read the manual – *The Sex Worker's Guide to Not Screwing Up Her Business 101* – is a real fucking no-no. A good sex worker *never* blurs the line between client and boyfriend.

Mr Sheffield was about ten years older than me, charismatic, charming and an absolute Adonis: slicked-back hair with a sprinkling of silver at the temples, glasses, expensive suit and the natural tan of someone who makes a lot of international trips. But it wasn't just that. I'd been completely cunt-dazzled by the fact that he'd made me cum. Sometimes a client requests that I squirt (which costs extra) and I *can* make myself cum during a booking, but only with the help of high-voltage toys and only if I can successfully tune out the other person. With Mr Sheffield, it was all him. Every cell in my body was drawn to him like the tide to the moon. My orgasms didn't need no power tools.

For a sex worker, it's good that your sex drive gets this kind of howdy every now and then, because when you have sex for a living the effect on your desire can be numbing. If I really pull back on the number of clients I see – like, just a couple of overnights a month – my horndog self does creep back, because I'm able to remember what I genuinely enjoy rather than moulding myself to fit someone else's fantasies. But with Mr Sheffield the sheer force of our erotic connection had my libido firing on command.

Initially, he'd booked me through my website. In his messages he came across as polite and cordial. I was in Sydney for a tour and he was one of my first clients. I was in a rush that day, having to jump out of the cab at the hotel, check in and get in the shower all within about ten minutes, because he would arrive in the lobby at any second.

I'd decided to go budget, picking a place that had serviced apartments so that I could spread my shit out over multiple rooms. So when I went down to the lobby, he looked out of place. This guy was super attractive and refined. He was no Booking.com Genius deal, put it like that. Immediately I wanted to apologise for making him come to that place.

The moment we got the admin done – cash, shower – it was on. This man was beautiful. He smelled incredible. I'd happily have let him rub himself all over me without taking a shower. When he fucked me he had a way of taking control that was firm but fair. He wasn't into slapping and choking – those porn-informed actions that so many clients seemed to think was required of them – but he did know how to handle me confidently, navigating my curves like he was driving a Porsche on a hairpin road. He delayed his own orgasm by periodically hitting pause to eat me out. I came three times and didn't charge him a single cent for my copious squirting, since I couldn't take the credit. Before our session was done, I was mentally speed-dialling Eden to tell her every single detail.

Afterwards, we lounged on the bed and talked. We went overtime but I didn't mention the idea of extending for extra. As long as we could order Uber Eats so that I could refuel before the next client, I was more than happy to have him stick around.

We related to each other on so many levels, beginning with the foundation of temperament and humour. Our birthdays were two days apart, making us both Cancers, and we both had ADHD and took the same meds. We were both parents and had similar values when it came to raising kids.

As with a lot of clients, he'd followed my work for a long time and was well versed in Kayla Jade, from my porn videos to every thought I'd ever expressed on Instagram. I pointed out that this gave him the advantage because he knew more about me than I did him. He lay back, his hands behind his head, and said I could ask him anything I liked.

'Are you still with the mum of your kids?' I asked, trying to make it sound like I was teasing rather than genuinely interested. Without hesitation, he replied that he was separated. I felt my heart rate spike in a way that was 100 per cent high school – a genuine excitement that I thought this job had drummed out of me. But, then, I only had his word for it. Also, men have very flexible definitions of 'separated'.

When he finally got up to leave, I made a move. I told him that I was in Sydney on tour for five days, but that my final day was free. Should we go out somewhere? For a split second, my suggestion hung in the balance. I got the panicked thought that his face would suddenly distort into a laugh, or into disgust. *Is this a* date? *With a* sex worker?

'Let's do it,' he said, smiling. 'We could meet here and I'll surprise you.'

~

If you think dating can be confusing – *are we an item, are we not?* – consider my predicament. Over the next few months I saw Mr Sheffield a lot. Either we'd hang out for a whole weekend when I came to Sydney, or he'd fly to the Gold Coast just to see me. Whenever we met, no money would change hands, but he would semi-regularly drop money into my account on *other* days, without any preamble or explanation.

Was it that he genuinely wanted to date me, but didn't want to be presumptuous? Or did it mean these were bookings but he was trying not to be crass about it by handing over a wad of cash? If you've ever become a forensic detective and spent days trying to analyse a guy's last message, sending screenshots to various friends for their counsel, try to wrap your head around Mr Sheffield's irregular deposits into my bank account. This was way more of a headfuck than what I experienced before I got into sex work: seeing a guy I was into mark himself as in a 'situationship' or declare 'it's complicated'. Something prevented me from asking Mr Sheffield his intentions outright: probably the fear of disappointment.

Without fail, the dates he organised required a lot of thought. He'd get a reservation at a restaurant with a three-month wait list, or book us into a brand-new boutique hotel that had been getting great reviews. Unlike most guys I met, he always asked me lots of questions about myself, but also respected my boundaries – what was left of them, anyway.

In between dates, we messaged constantly. I gave him my personal number, rather than my work number, and every time my phone buzzed, my clit twinged. It was like my phone and my pussy were in psychic communication. Every time I had an orgasm – either with him or when I was alone, thinking of him – the endorphins served as positive reinforcement. My physiological response to Mr Sheffield was rewiring my brain to become ever more obsessed. His name – his real name – was the first thought in my head when I woke up and the last before I fell asleep. This shit was scary.

I looked forward to our banter and chats just as much as the sex. As if I was his girlfriend, he debriefed to me about his day at work and the ridiculous workplace dynamics and gossip. As a sole trader, I missed out on that kind of drama and gossip, so I found it genuinely fascinating. I did notice that he gave fewer details of his friends, family and ex-partner, but then, I always kept those things secret, too.

One Sunday afternoon, as we lounged by a hotel pool, Mr Sheffield said he wanted to take me to the Maldives. This kind of offer wasn't new to me. I'm alert to the tone in which they're offered, and the timing. Usually it's a guy big-noting, flushed by a session in which I've systematically boosted his ego. He'd love me to know that he could just click his fingers and whisk me off, take care of me – no expense spared. But this felt different. Mr Sheffield told me about his previous trip there, years ago, about the dolphin and whale tours he'd been on. He knew I goddamn loved whale watching. So, he said, could I block off a week and join him? The idea of being able to completely chill and get to know him, rather than having to bookend our dates with appointments with other men, was even more appealing than the ultra-exclusive, whale-laden, luxury beach holiday aspect – honest to god. We started to make plans, me resting my head on his shoulder as we scrolled through accommodation options.

To let the feeling of love and possibility expand my chest felt liberating. It felt as though we were meant to be, but every now and then I was plagued by doubt. The trickery of my job is I know exactly how to talk the talk with clients and make them feel like they're having a magical connection. Maybe I'd met my match in Mr Sheffield. Maybe he was just as good at fuelling a fantasy as me. And since he wasn't a sex worker, did that simply make him a narcissist? People with that personality disorder are experts at love-bombing. They'll seem to share the exact same interests as you. They'll reflect back at you what you want to see. It'll blow your mind how ideal they are for you. And then they turn.

Either way, the dates for that trip to the Maldives kept on changing and changing, and never getting any closer.

~

When Mr Sheffield and I first started seeing each other, I didn't have a lot of clout. By the time he'd been wooing me for a year, I had two million followers on TikTok. Every time I went out to a bar or restaurant, women would approach me, wanting a photo or to say hi. Even if they just had questions about my skincare routine, Mr Sheffield would get the side-eye because they would have heard enough of my stories to want to start guessing: was this one of the dudes I regularly posted about?

Mr Sheffield had already told me that one day he'd been in the break room at work when two women were gossiping about me. He 'innocently' asked what they were talking about (oh, begone, my pang of jealousy) and they showed him my TikTok account, fingering the phone screen for ever more salacious videos. He laughed as he recounted this. But I sensed tension.

Increasingly, I noticed that my fame was stressing him out, particularly in Sydney – his home turf. I don't know why, since by now I had every one of my millions of female followers completely in love with him too. Maybe he was just antsy about being seen or pictured with a sex worker from the point of view of his professional reputation, but my spidey senses were going off. Was the real problem that he wasn't single and that someone who knew his girlfriend – or wife – would spot us out?

One major red flag was that he barely had any online presence. In this day and age, that usually means somebody's shady and has something to hide. I knew he was following me on Instagram because he always knew what I'd been talking about on that platform, but I couldn't figure out which account was his and I was too cool to ask. Stalking someone online is a slippery slope anyway. I didn't want to go down the rabbit hole of trying to find his house on Google Earth and seeing if there was another person's car in the drive.

When we met up I'd only get a couple of hours' sleep because of all the sex and talking, and then I'd start getting dark and overanalysing as soon as he had gone, because fatigue will do that to you.

One night, we went out to a beautiful restaurant and had the perfect evening. I found myself typing our conversations into my phone every time he went to the bathroom so that I could be sure I'd never forget. Back at the hotel, we screwed and talked till 3am. I was starting to doze off when a noise woke me. Mr Sheffield was stepping into his pants. *Leaving.* Some long-dead ghost of rejection came back from my teenage years in Palmy, from seeing a guy I'd crushed on for ages leave in the night after we finally fucked. I couldn't even remember the guy, but that feeling of betrayal knifed my heart anew.

'Where are you going?' I asked, clinging on to some insane hope that he was getting ice for drinks or making sure he hadn't left his headlights on.

Mr Sheffield whispered, as if to try and soothe me back to sleep. He had to leave because of an early start at work. He wanted to let me sleep now rather than wake me in the morning. It seemed super-suss to me, but I was still being the cool girl.

'Drive safe,' I said, and turned away to hug my pillow.

Sleep evaded me for hours, and then the insomnia bled into weeks. In my angrier moments, I wondered if I should start billing him again, but I couldn't mentally write myself a script that didn't seem childish. I also had to acknowledge that during that week I'd posted some stories on my Instagram that made it clear that I'd packed in a lot of clients on that Sydney trip. He would have seen those stories, for sure. Maybe he was paying me back.

My friends had a theory: Mr Sheffield was a) taken and b) addicted to sex workers. Maybe he was even a collector. If that was the case, I didn't understand why he would have to lie about it. I'd asked him outright what his status was and he'd sworn he was single.

Sidebar: if you want my best advice for getting a shady guy to tell the truth, ask him a direct question, such as, 'Where were you last night?' or 'How many other sex workers are you seeing?' or 'Did you ever have any intention to really take me to the Maldives?' Then when he gives his minimalist, mumbled answer, you pause. Don't respond. He'll scramble to fill the silence because it's fucking awkward. Keep that up and you'll dig down to the real gold.

After that trip to Sydney, I decided to pull the plug. I let Mr Sheffield know that I'd be available for bookings but that I wouldn't see him casually anymore and that I wouldn't be available to chat. He messaged back that he understood – gutting – and that he'd be in touch next time I was in town. I had to respect that. He didn't owe me anything, and I hadn't asked for anything. It was just that seeing Mr Sheffield felt like driving a car and not knowing what was in your blind spot. It's unnerving, and you know it's probably not safe.

~

Over the next few months I only had occasional contact with Mr Sheffield while I licked my wounds. It was silly, because if he'd pledged his undying love for me I would have had to bounce anyway because I wasn't ready to give up the job. While I know a few sex workers who have married a client and had kids, the reality is usually that a partner will get jealous, resentful or controlling – like, you can see *this* client but not *that* one – or will start making up their own rules so that they can see other people. Don't even get me started on the insecurity when you make more money than them. So why did I even care? By giving Mr Sheffield the flick we'd both dodged a bullet.

No relationship ends neatly, though, so I don't need to tell you that we had one last fling, months later. Mr Sheffield was obviously still studying my Instagram like an A-grade student, because he knew I was coming to Sydney. He offered dinner at the one restaurant we'd both absolutely loved – a super-exclusive place that basically offered three dishes and if you didn't like steak, that was your problem. They even confiscated your phone on arrival so that filthy rich people didn't have to worry about pesky influencers trying to Gram the place.

For four hours, we picked up exactly where we left off: the in-jokes, the genuine interest, the office-gossip updates.

Back at the hotel we had sex and he made me come three times. He always insisted I go for that third title even when I was sure I couldn't manage it: 'A quitter never wins and a winner never quits,' he'd say. He was always right. Afterwards, we lay in each other's arms. I bit the bullet and told him I really liked him. He said he felt the same way. I quizzed him on his relationship status and he admitted that he'd been seeing someone in the early days, but that it hadn't been serious. I didn't enquire as to the exact definition of 'early days', nor did I necessarily believe he was single now. While we'd always have that beautiful night, I had to accept that I'd never completely trust him – and that wasn't any way to live.

When he followed up the next afternoon to see if we could catch up one more time before I left, I told him no way. I had my mum in town and she was my priority. Sorry dude, another time. And you know where to find me – through my website.

Were my own trust issues sabotaging this love affair? Maybe. But we would not be making this mistake again.

Kayla Jade: Cultural Oddity

You know what's an awkward phone call? Your husband's gran, telling you she's seen your face next to a giant black cock. Who knew grannies were on X these days? Maybe she had help from Jackson's relo, the one who outed me by sending the family screenshots from my OnlyFans, which he'd taken the time to subscribe to.

This was the grandmother whose pale blue Mercedes Jackson drove me around in when we first met, so I had a soft place for her in my heart. Thankfully, as it turned out, Granny was far more at peace with my harlotry than that relative. She's a strict Catholic, forever busying herself with the local church, but she's also conscious that a woman needs to set herself up financially. I mean, about four years into my OnlyFans odyssey, her grandson got to move into a three-storey dream home, so it wasn't all that bad.

'In case you didn't know, it's on the internet,' Granny had said, a little sternly, but from then on she kept her disapproval to herself. It sounded like she'd secretly had quite a fun afternoon shocking herself at the snail trail of Kayla Jade she'd found on the internet, each discovery no doubt prompting a new gasp.

Within a year of that conversation, I started to be featured in mainstream media, including shows on the ABC and SBS. We're talking the kind of terrestrial TV and national radio stalwarts that Granny could approve of. These media networks seemed to give me a newfound legitimacy in the world, even though I was still doing what I'd always done. And then the brand deals came a-knocking. Even when I just casually used a product that I liked during my 'get ready with me' videos, the brand in question would find its popularity rocket without us having had any prior conversation. When I sprayed myself with my favourite Gem coconut and vanilla deodorant and noted, 'You can get a whole lot closer to a man's wallet when you smell good', that product sold out nationwide. And when I sampled a serum sent to me by Boring Without You, the company earned more than $100,000 in revenue over a few days. The owner, Davey Rooney, clapped back at pearl-clutchers who commented that its association with me was a 'bad move'. He told News.com.au, 'Sex work is fundamentally an issue of bodily autonomy, and every individual has the right to choose how they use their body and labour without being subjected to stigma or judgement.'

When I first started out, I never envisaged crossing over to the mainstream. I did know that some news sites had a taste for OnlyFans stories, because canny creators such as Honey Brooks were managing to get articles written about them. Sex workers are naturally good at marketing – we have to adapt to be the dream girl for every client, after all. At first I was just getting those kind of titillating takes from tabloids, who loved to churn my latest TikTok video and occasionally hit me up for a comment, but around eighteen months into my full-service sex work the interest shifted to a wider media audience, which had a domino effect. Suddenly I was being interviewed on current affairs shows, money podcasts, feminist podcasts, news shows – and these were *serious* interviews, about building my brand, and safety in full-service sex work. It was as though I was offering the ordinary world its first look behind the curtain of sex work, even though there have been incredible sex workers who have written memoirs and spoken publicly before me. What's novel about me is the sheer size of my female following, making it clear that we have entered a new era, where the world's oldest profession is finally becoming accepted as a valid career move. The lines between OnlyFans creators, influencers and entrepreneurs have become increasingly blurred. (On that, if you think sex work sounds exhausting, try creating high-quality content for the algorithm on a daily basis.)

The way I've played the media game is by being as open as possible, but also by being very careful. There are certain tricks of the trade that you can reveal and certain things that other sex workers would see as breaking a code. Similarly, there's a fine line between providing exciting stories and promoting sex work. I know the interviewer's TV network, or publisher, or radio station will insist that they provide *balance*, cautioning the public that sex work has its dangers and its critics, so that caution might as well come from me.

Slowly but surely, my own family have got used to my new-found fame. We're from a conservative town and I'm pretty sure they hadn't even visited a strip club before, so I get that it was hard to wrap their heads around this billion-dollar industry called OnlyFans, which has seen millions of enterprising young folk pose in the nuddy. In the early days, Mum was constantly telling me – with some relief and a touch of satisfaction – that she'd now found out that so-and-so's daughter was on

OnlyFans too. Undoubtedly you yourself know some creators, even if you don't *know* you do. Your barista, the guy two desks over, your niece … like, we walk among you.

Gradually Mum relaxed, particularly when she came over to stay with me and saw how happy I was. Jackson and I were no longer struggling – or arguing – and we were spending so much time with our kids. Dad never got angry. He said, 'Do whatever makes you happy' – but while that sounds really zen, it probably says more about his lack of commitment to anything in life. Dad's an old hand at just shrugging things off. My brother took the attitude that he was in no place to judge, having made some questionable life decisions, and so we've never gone deep. My big sister was a lot more resistant. She was worried for me, and worried for Mum's feelings, and for what people would think of us as a family. We didn't talk for a while, but we worked through it. I doubt the awards I've won for my porn work are framed on her wall, but at the same time if she mentions my name to someone now she'll probably just get, 'Oh, I think I've seen her on TikTok!' rather than anything more salacious.

My family know there are two Kayla Jades. One makes deadpan TikTok videos about BV. The other is wholesome as fuck. I'm serious: my home smells like a day spa and vanilla muffins. It's spotless. I'm obsessed with the birdlife in my garden, I keep chickens, I'm ruled by my cats. If I have visitors, I'm quick to serve the kind of smorgasbord of beautiful snacks that Meghan Markle or Martha Stewart would be proud of. I'm always 100 per cent switched *on* the moment my kids walk through the front door after school. It's pure cottagecore.

I started to wonder how I could present both these worlds to the public. In the early days I'd talk about how much money I made and

I'd count my cash. People loved those videos. They found it relaxing, watching my acrylic nails shuffle through green and yellow notes. But then one video titled 'Day in my life', where I counted cash, really blew up, getting 5.4 million views. That shook me a bit. I could tell from the comments that some were young women who were intrigued by the idea of sex work, assuming they could make this kind of cold hard cash 'easily'.

Nothing about sex work is easy. First off, you have to be a shrewd businesswoman. Part of my success was launching on OnlyFans at exactly the right time during the pandemic when people were really getting interested in the platform – and that ship has sailed for the next gen of girls. The market has become saturated and it's way harder to break through. There's also a huge emotional cost and personal sacrifice that comes with being a sex worker, not to mention the danger, and I didn't want to be responsible for anyone making the decision to start. So, even though it had become my signature, I decided to stop counting cash in my videos. The video where I announced my decision to do that only got 2.3 million views. Meh. You win some, you lose some.

Instead, I tentatively started answering more questions about the arrangement I have with Jackson – because people are *obsessed* with getting glimpses of Baby Daddy, always commenting whenever there's a tiny snippet of his voice left in one of my video edits (oh, whoops). I gave tours of the wild bushland of my property, introduced my cats, gave updates on my baby chicks hatching. Turns out people *can* hold two truths in their head in one time – that a woman can be a sex worker and a wholesome gal – and I felt a huge weight off my shoulders as these separate versions of me started gliding towards each other and finally became one. If you've ever felt you had to hide parts of yourself in relationships and then you meet someone who completely accepts every aspect of you, you'll know what I mean.

With this interest growing from mainstream media, I decided to launch my own podcast, *Storytime with Kayla Jade*. A month in, we had a million streams. Six weeks in, 2 million. This show is entirely aimed at the girlies, who make up about 95 per cent of my army of TikTok followers. On TikTok, rather than talk *at* people, I've always tried to chat *to* them, like we're having a cocktail together (helped by the fact that I'm often making a cocktail at the same time, or tucking into some charcuterie snacks). That's not contrived – I started off making these videos for the amusement of my fellow sex workers, and the wider audience naturally evolved. Women relate to the jaded, slightly salty tone when I discuss my clients; we're just talking about men, after all.

The podcast is lighter, like a proper girly catch-up where you lounge on the sofa and spill the tea. The topics roam all over the place depending on my mood. Sometimes I lift the lid on the sex industry with guest creators such as Girthmaster, Angela White and Eden Lux; sometimes there's a deep-and-meaningful, like about my eating disorder years, or about my feelings about having people discuss my kids online. I found I really enjoyed being a host – the process of researching a guest, interviewing them and making that interview sound like a natural chat. I learn fast and I like thinking on my feet.

Girthmaster said something really interesting about fame when he came on the show. When he went viral a few years back, after being profiled as 'the internet's boyfriend' in *Rolling Stone* and getting a shout-out on X from Cardi B, he materialised on hundreds of millions of people's radars overnight. Established porn star Owen Gray reached out to him and pointed out that Girth was experiencing in one week the kind of attention that most people in the industry had years to acclimatise to. Owen said to only pay attention to what was being said by the people who *knew* him.

That really chimed with me, because I'd had to rehaul my thinking about public opinion. On the daily I'm tagged in video after video of people giving their shitty hot takes on me, and it's stressful. Right from the start I made the decision not to respond, because that's what they want – it just gives them more content – but at the same time, I found my attention was drawn to what they were saying, monitoring chats where my name was running hot. It's so hard not to buy into the drama. I've been criticised for glamorising the industry, for going to a group dinner with the rapper Drake (I had no idea there had been allegations made about him) and for supposedly being an absent mum, because my kids aren't in my videos. It smacks of desperation. If I was just starting out on a platform and my page was doing badly, I'd never stoop so low as to try to get views by trashing someone else and trying to glom onto that person's following. By doing these shitty broadcasts about sex workers they get to profit from sex work without experiencing any of the stigma. Good for them, hey?

It's nice to have normal friends outside of the industry to de-frazzle with: people who are barely even on social media. Our brains weren't designed for this level of intake of other people's opinions. Jackson advises me to compartmentalise, to see Kayla Jade as a persona, but it's hard not to take criticism personally when it's my face out there and my real name that people are using. We try to laugh about it together, because if we didn't laugh, I'd cry.

Apart from those little blips that are out of my control, I'm incredibly happy about the brand I've built. Even though I only average one client a week now and make most of my money online, my business has grown exponentially. If I wasn't the figurehead for this multi-million-dollar brand I'd never even know about the haters. Does the CEO of Coca-Cola sweat the reviews on Trustpilot? Doubt it.

I recently found an old photograph that made me feel really sad for my younger self. I'm about sixteen years old, on a trip to Australia with my family. We're at Australia Zoo, taking turns holding a koala. At first glance, I look confident: my long hair is dyed a defiant scarlet, my sunnies are perched on top of my head and I'm smiling. But I couldn't enjoy a moment of this holiday because my negative self-talk was so loud that it was like a huge secret, driving a wedge between me and my family. I was there, but I wasn't there – you know what I mean? I was scared – scared of food, scared of showing that I was scared, scared that my life was pointless. If you told me back then that I could be as happy as I am now, I would never have believed you. I had no plan, no direction, nothing figured out. That's why it bugs me when well-meaning people are desperate to know my next move. Media mogul? TV host? Launch a clothes line? Move to LA?

Here's something that I wish people would discuss more: it's totally okay to not know what you're doing – not just when you're a kid, but when you're an adult. Life is so random and unpredictable. Anything interesting could happen at any point; we don't need the pressure of plotting out a five-year plan if that's not our jam. All the times I've hustled my ass off have been spur-of-the-moment decisions. I've had a natural instinct to push in a certain direction, and if I see results, I keep on pushing. This photo reminded me that we literally have no idea how our lives are going to turn out. There could be exciting stuff just waiting around the corner. So be kind to yourself and keep moving forward.

What I'm Teaching My Kids

It was a hot day, so I'd got us all an ice cream. Katie was on my hip, having decided she could no longer walk. Benji was keeping up a refrain of 'Mummy? Mummy? Mummy?', eager to tell me about his new Minecraft side-plots. As I tapped my card I spotted a woman in her twenties waiting at the next checkout along, angling her phone at me. I was used to people papping pictures, but so far no photos of my kids had wound up online. I wanted to go full Björk on her and whale her to the ground, but I kept my cool. I didn't want Katie or Benji sussing that anything was wrong. I don't want *anything* pulling them out of their carefree world.

When people ask if I fear being judged as a parent, they forget one thing: I became a parent at twenty-one. I've *always* been judged. Jackson, too. We found it alienating hanging around older parents in toddlers' groups and at swimming dates. It just made our bond all the tighter. I probably shouldn't admit it, but most parents seemed boring to us. Some parents in their forties gravitated to us when we were in our twenties, wanting to hang out and drink, but then they'd find out we weren't big partyers and they'd drift off, disappointed. We were forever on the fringes, and that suited us.

I always knew I wanted kids. I get really triggered by any story in the news about something happening to a child. I don't know if it's my ADHD or if it's because I'm a Cancer – we're generally super empathetic – but if I read a story like that, I will feel so much pain and I'll constantly be thinking about it. I had so much love to give and, like Jackson, I had my own ideas of how to raise children – which were perfectly aligned with his. No shade on our parents, but we wanted a gentler approach, one where the kids are given as much respect as the adults.

Benji's and Katie's births weirdly reflected their very different personalities. If Benji comes up against a problem, he'll patiently find a way to figure it out. He was born on a stormy night in Palmerston North. It was the middle of the night and I couldn't stop vomiting. I loved having a baby inside me, even though I was sick throughout my pregnancies. I was super hippie, adapting to a vegan diet like Jackson's, and insisting on no drugs when the time came. And the time had obviously come.

I woke up Jackson, went to the bathroom to puke again, then we grabbed the go-bag and went to the hospital. It was 1am and pelting rain outside, but we managed to make it there in one piece. I'd wanted a water birth, but when the time came I couldn't face sitting up. Lying on my back on a bed was the only position I could handle. I was restless, agitated. Jackson fed me jelly beans to keep my energy up and I would hit them out of his hands because he kept giving me black ones when he knows I hate them.

Benji was facing the wrong way. He wasn't breeched but he was spine to spine with me, which meant he would have to corkscrew when he came out. We managed to avoid forceps because he twisted himself around naturally, but the whole process was agonising. I had my legs up in stirrups and was doing tug of war with the midwife, holding a towel, because that's how you push the baby out. I was yelling, 'Get me an epidural!' but she knew that I'd been adamant that I wasn't having drugs, so she talked me out of it. When Benji was born, at 10.15am, he had a cone head from all that swivelling.

'Is my baby gonna stay like that?' I asked the midwife as she laid him on my chest. But I already loved him to bits. *I'll put a beanie on him*, I thought. *He'll be all right.*

Maybe because of the corkscrewing he had to do to come into this world, Benji is a flexible kid. He can shift his attitude to accommodate someone else's point of view, and he's super chill. He has to be, with Katie as a sister.

Katie came two years later, and her birth was like a madcap comedy movie. This time, Jackson and I had been doing hypnobirthing classes and had a doula. By now we were living on the Sunshine Coast in Queensland, so when shit kicked off, Jackson's mum raced up from the Gold Coast to watch Benji for us.

I started getting contractions while we were watching *When Harry Met Sally*, which was good, because that movie really sucked. I was insistent that these spasms were just Braxton Hicks. Sounds like a shit band, but it's actually phantom contractions that act almost like a practice run, to get the body ready for the idea of giving birth. Katie was already so late that they thought she might have to be induced, but my ethos was *she'll come when she's ready*. I had a TENS machine, which shocks you with little currents to help with the pain, but when the intensity increased I switched that for a bath.

After a while, Jackson insisted that we go to hospital. In the car, one contraction was so gnarly that I wanted to scream, but we hadn't yet handed Benji over to Jackson's mum, so I had to hold back my reactions to avoid scaring him.

When we reached the hospital, I got out of the car and just lay on the ground. We were still trying to play it cool with Benji, like it was all a fun game. Jackson ran off with him to get a wheelchair so that we could wheel Mummy along. By this point Jackson's mum had arrived and was pegging it from the parking lot to the hospital. We saw her sprinting through the aerobridge, and then halfway across she spotted me, sprawled out on the tarmac. It was like a slapstick film, watching her bang on the glass as I rolled around on the ground.

By the time Jackson and Benji came back with the wheelchair, numerous people had walked straight past me sprawled out on the ground, and not a single one asked if I was okay. I was surprised no one threw some loose change. Jackson and Benji wheeled me into the hospital, right up to the birthing suite, bursting in through the double doors just as his mum skidded around the corner. Jackson went to draw me a bath but it had only filled to ankle deep when I said, 'The baby's coming!'

The nurses were patronising me, telling me she *wasn't* coming and that they knew it was painful but that I should just chill out.

'She's *coming*,' I told them, pretty fucking emphatically. They took a look and jumped to attention. I'd waited so long at home thinking that my labour was just Braxton Hicks that I was now way further into the real deal than we had thought.

Within five minutes, Katie popped out. I actually birthed her myself, grabbing her out of my vagina and putting her on my chest.

'Don't touch my baby! She's MY baby!' I yelled, when the nurses tried to clean her up.

Ever since that day, Katie has reliably turned up late and on her own terms. Sometimes she struggles with routine and keeping her space tidy, but since she was diagnosed with ADHD we've been given practical ways to deal with that. Ultimately, we want Katie to be Katie: smart, sassy and hilarious. Whenever we watch a movie or cartoon where there's a popular girl villain, *that's* the character Katie identifies with. We'll try to explain that this character is a metaphor for certain negative things, but what can I say – my kid knows her own mind. She's so like me that I know any trick she might want to pull. She also loves performing and is preoccupied with beauty, even though I hardly wear make-up at home. She always wants to pose in the mirror and play with my products. I tell her, 'You're so beautiful, why would you want to put anything on your face?'

Amid the chaos there's one sweet-hearted girl. Katie's a ball of energy and she just lights up whenever she talks. I'm a little in awe of her.

If I'm more like Katie, Jackson is definitely more like Benji. Our son is very empathetic, very kind, very caring. He's gonna make an incredible husband one day. His teachers constantly email me about how well he is doing and Jackson thinks one of them is a little obsessed with him. I don't blame her. Benji is outgoing, but also a little anxious, because he's a critical thinker like Jackson, weighing up every possibility.

Jackson thinks it's good that we're so different as parents, because it means our kids can't just rebel against their old folks like we're one homogenous unit. They're going to have to be really specific if they want to challenge us. The through-line between all four of us is that we have the exact same sense of humour. If there were cameras in the house to record the goofy way we interact, people would probably find it ridiculous. We lean very heavily into silliness. We watch absurd videos together. We're all learning piano. Maybe it comes down to us being young parents. While I get on really well with my mum, we don't share the same humour or cultural references.

But we can also draw the line. We never wanted to be those parents who can't go to restaurants because they have kids. We've taken Benji and Katie everywhere from day one, training them to behave well out in public. Cuffing your kid around the head was more normalised when I was growing up, so we are very conscious of gentle parenting, of talking to a kid rather than punishing them. That doesn't mean we're pushovers – we have really strong boundaries and we're very direct – but because we don't shut down our kids' conversations, they respect us and they know that when we get firmer, we really mean it.

Our kids can really feel that closeness between us. When a parent's job means they only see their kid for an hour a night, they miss out on so much. It's not that every conversation has to be a life lesson or something profound, but we are still connecting with them all the time. That's such a different environment to the way I was raised, with parents whose work, out of necessity, meant that time with them was scarce; or Jackson's family, who he doesn't spend much time with. Despite the fact that I make weird-ass martinis for the TikTok clout, Jackson and I very rarely drink. Our parents' generation need to be constantly drinking, for some reason, and if you don't join in they act like it's rude. Sometimes it's easier to just give in, but we're pretty naturally energetic and we don't need to loosen up.

For those who 'worry' that me having a BBL and spending money on my appearance might have a negative effect on our kids, consider that Jackson grew up on the Gold Coast, where so much weight is put on image and status, but has always chosen to be a humble guy. We're emphasising to our kids that no matter what we choose to look like on the outside, it's important to nurture a genuine sense of self.

Jackson managed to find a friendship group that was anti that kind of superficiality. Ironically, the way to rebel on the Gold Coast is by *not* drinking or doing drugs, so Jackson was straight edge in high school. When everyone started getting heavily into partying in their mid-teens, he'd watch them slur and stagger around and feel repelled. He found his tribe of kids who drew Xs on their hands to represent straight edge, and he got into the bands and the ideology.

Now that Benji is getting a little bit older, we're able to show him more music videos and Jackson has introduced him to some of his straight-edge favourites. That became an in-road to talk to our kids about why a lot of their favourite rappers died young – because they took too many drugs. We don't ever want Benji to get swept up with whatever the crowd is doing. We're teaching him to be confident and to be himself, even if that sometimes puts him at odds with people. Self-expression is an act of rebellion. Respecting women is also an act of rebellion. Benji definitely questions authority. I'm really glad about that. He questions everything.

When Katie gets a bit older I'll advise her to put herself first. I wasted so much energy obsessing about boys and their needs, putting them on pedestals. I was practically in a cult of my own making. That was energy

I could have funnelled into developing my own identity. I want Katie to feel sure of her own worth.

~

The question I get asked the most is: *What are you going to tell your kids?*

Our kids know I do TikTok. They'll see me filming the chickens or eating a cute cake for the camera. But I'm very careful with what I say around them. I say that I go out with people as a kind of glamorous entertainer. I make it clear that it's my job, that I get paid, so that they know I would prefer to be having fun with them. They're both such open-minded kids. I don't think it really affects their day to day. They go to a private school and both their homeroom teachers are lovely to me. They know who I am. They're always mentioning one TikTok video or another. People love to live vicariously. A few mums at the school gates have sidled up to me and said, 'I'm in the wrong business!'

There have also been plenty of folk who I've heard on the grapevine have been judgemental, and then there are the people who Jackson thinks want to be friends with me because then they'll have anecdotes for their *other* friends. In any case, we've found our tight friends over time, and they're people from all walks of life, with open minds.

So when people ask: *What are you going to do when your kids grow up and they find out you're a sex worker?* I say this: first of all, I teach them to not be judgemental. I teach them love. I teach them kindness and empathy. I've always taught them to love people for who they are, no matter what their situation. If people care so much about my kids potentially getting bullied for what their mother does, how about they focus on teaching their own kids not to be judgemental? I trust that when my kids look back on their lives, they're not going to be focusing on the fact that I was a sex worker; they'll be remembering all the wonderful memories, the trips, the care. Being a present mother means so much more to children than what you do for a job.

My Idea of Romance

He wanted to order off-menu for me – he reckoned I'd love the wagyu. He wanted to give me a wad of cash in the casino afterwards and watch me attempt the blackjack table (but only for one game, and then he just wanted me to watch *him* do it better). He wanted me to call him Daddy. The dude was my age, but sure.

Andrew wore Gucci pants and Yeezy slides. His sunglasses were Louis Vuitton. His watch, Richard Mille. A brand whore, then, but I wasn't about to judge a whore. Wherever we went – Melbourne's hottest restaurants, which he must have booked way in advance, though each time he claimed to know a guy – he insisted on taking pictures for the Gram. It made me cringe. These just weren't the kinds of places you whipped out your phone. Since *he* was doing it, though, sometimes I'd film a quick 'Everything I Ate At …' for TikTok.

Andrew was okay-looking, but he was dead behind the eyes. Nothing impressed him or seemed to give him any enjoyment. Perhaps that's why he kept seeking more and more stimulation. His game was crypto and he was always giving me investment advice for free. He was harmless, though, so I was angling on keeping him as a regular Melbourne client. He was easy money.

On our fourth booking, Andrew requested an overnight. He chose the hotel, too; one attached to the casino. We ate at a two-hatted restaurant in the city, because he wanted to fuck me in the toilet. As usual, he ordered for me before I could get a word in. Happily, he included a bottle of Cristal.

'Is Dizzy working today?' he asked the waiter. 'Amazing. Tell him Andrew says hi.'

Poker-faced, she nodded and returned to the kitchen.

'Head chef,' Andrew explained. I nodded. 'Great guy.'

Over dinner, Andrew told me he had a trip to Hong Kong coming up and wanted to take me with him. We'd stay at the Rosewood and eat at Caprice. He was vague on the dates. Andrew kept disappearing to the men's room, presumably to do a bump, and I kept topping up his glass with Cristal so that he bought another bottle. Before long, his promise to fuck me in the toilet was forgotten. After he paid the bill, we awkwardly held hands as we walked back to the hotel.

'I've got a surprise for you,' he said, and I tried to sound excited.

Up in the suite, Andrew asked if I'd heard of *wakamezake*. He had to repeat it a few times because he was slurring. I laughingly told him as much and he did another bump.

'The Japanese do it,' he said, now standing in only his Versace Greca Border trunks (which his mother had probably ironed). He produced another bottle of Cristal that had been chilling in the fridge. Good – my mission was to get this guy out cold as quickly as possible.

'Lie down,' he said, 'and keep your legs closed.' I pulled off my g-string and settled on the bed, and he poured the Cristal over my crotch so that it pooled between the tops of my thighs. If I'd known, I would have put down a towel. He got on all fours on the bed and started lapping at the liquid, his belly weighed down by gravity. Andrew had never gone to town on me so I guessed this was the nearest he was prepared to venture.

'Oh my god,' I said gamely. 'Fuccck!'

He snorted in approval and kept lapping until all the liquid had gone, which took longer than you might expect. He looked a bit unsure for a moment, then pushed my legs open so that he could kneel between them. We both looked down as he pressed his floppy helmet aimlessly at my vulva.

Coke dick.

'We could try later,' I said, hoping he'd do another bump and really fuck himself. He agreed. The next hour passed in an excruciating montage of failed positions and swigging of Cristal. Eventually he brought the empty bottle to my pussy and started trying to nudge the tip in.

'*No,*' I said firmly, pushing his arm away. He shrugged and gave up. The guy slept the peaceful sleep of those without a moral compass.

~

There was one thing that was extremely unusual about this booking, and it wasn't Andrew's wardrobe. On the previous three occasions, he had transferred the whole payment into my account upfront. This time, I got uncharacteristically slack and took his word for it. There was one point, halfway through dinner, when Andrew was doing a bump in the toilets, that I remembered I should check, but when I picked up my phone to open my banking app, I got distracted by a message from a friend.

After he left the next morning I finally checked the app and realised to my horror that he hadn't transferred anything. He owed me $12,000 for the overnight stay, plus the cost of the hotel suite, which I'd booked. I immediately messaged him and he apologised, saying he'd transfer it immediately. Thirty minutes later, I messaged him again.

'It didn't go through?' he typed back.

After another thirty minutes of messaging, he was pointing out that he'd paid for the dinner and the Cristal, as if we were even. And then there was a change of tack: 'I'll get it to you,' he wrote. 'I have to transfer some bitcoin.'

'I don't take bitcoin,' I wrote back, 'and I don't do Afterpay.'

By now it was time to check out of the hotel, and I was raging. The idea of someone spending money they didn't have, let alone spending mine, made my head spin. Andrew probably rented his wardrobe on a monthly subscription plan, using maxed-out credit cards.

'I'll call the front desk and pay now,' Andrew wrote.

I knew he wouldn't, and I'd paid upfront anyway. Fuck this. It was time to call in the heavies – specifically, the bouncer that I have on speed-dial for absolute last resorts.

Look, Jackson's the nicest guy on the face of this earth, but if you fuck over someone he loves, he'll really go after you. Seeing me arrive home distraught, he kicked into gear. His dad was a loan shark in Pittsburgh in the States, so he'd learned the tough-guy act from the best.

When I first met Andrew I'd checked his driver's licence, so I knew where he lived. Jackson and I gave him twenty-four hours' grace to see if he'd transfer the money, and then we got to plotting a two-pronged attack.

Prong one: the little visit. Two days after the booking, we did a drive-by of Andrew's apartment, prepared to park and wait for him to get home from work ... although, where did one who 'does crypto' actually work? In any case, I'd brought snacks. When we pulled up further down the road, Andrew's car was there, so Jackson took a moment to get his head in the game, then ran up the steps of the apartment block. In one hand he gripped a—

Hold up, hold up, you don't need to say that.

Yeah, whoopsie, sorry. Yes, that's Jackson. He's like my personal cloud server, because thanks to my ADHD, I can hardly remember a damn thing about my life. He's had to remind me of the details of most of the events in this book, so I hope he's been telling the truth.

You could just say I knocked at the door.

Yeah, so he knocked at the door and Andrew answered. I was parked way down the road, the engine idling, trying to get a good view in the wing mirror. There was a lot of waving of hands and then Jackson gestured at a van parked nearby. Eventually Andrew shut the door and Jackson came swaggering back down the road, taking his time. When he got to the car he jumped in – *'Drive, drive, drive!'* – but he was creasing up, too. Jackson had made out that he had a whole bunch of mates waiting in that random van. Andrew nearly shit his Versace jocks. 'You've got three days,' Jackson told him, sticking a finger in his face, and then added some interest.

Prong two: the persuasion. Jackson reinforced the urgency by revealing some pertinent details he'd found out about Andrew, using his wily researcher skills (it's great that all those years at university have come in handy). He was able to tell Andrew where he worked, the name of his parents and the name of his ex-wife. Before the three-day deadline was up, Andrew had made the transfer. I wish him well with his crypto trading endeavours. But also, remember, son: the dildo of consequence rarely arrives lubed.

~

Have you seen *A Star Is Born*, where another Jackson – Jackson Maine – becomes increasingly jealous and insecure when his girlfriend's career takes off? Yeah, it's not like that with us. Jackson's my right-hand man. He does everything he can to contribute behind the scenes, from videography to podcast engineering to tech support to my personal security. We're a good team, but more than that: we see both our roles as investing in the family business.

It's the difference between paying rent and paying a mortgage. Or the difference between being with the kids and putting all my energy into working for someone else's business that I don't care about. I'm investing in our family, even if that's just chatting and laughing with the kids as I drive them to school.

Some of my regular clients have become jealous when they've found out about Jackson via the TikTok sleuths but, as for how Jackson feels, let's put him in the hot seat, rather than speculate. Jackson, how have you felt about my full-time harlotry?

My philosophy, inherited from my mother, is to feel the fear and do it anyway, so I just jumped in when you did. I put my own feelings aside, because I'd hate you to look back in a few years' time and think, damn, I wish I could have taken that trip to Greece with the A-Lister. I was never going to say, hmm, that sounds like a cool opportunity but it would make me uncomfortable. If I had, we'd both regret it now.

Our relationship got way better when we said, 'Fuck it, who cares?' and let go of what a traditional relationship should be. And in any case, raising kids together is much more of a commitment than marriage. When we were together-together we both had certain expectations of each other and we would get frustrated when they weren't met. By taking all that away we became two independent people again, who enjoy each other's company and make each other laugh. It's healthy to have the space to have your own separate identity and to not to have to depend on the other person to have all your needs met. After experiencing a relationship like this I could never go back to something traditional. I'm banned from all the dating apps, anyway, for using them as funnels to my social media accounts.

The one rule with us is honesty. Like, if I see a client, or if I film with someone, I tell Jackson just as I would my friends. He himself has no interest in appearing in my mattress-actress videos. We filmed a whole catalogue of those before I was even in this business, but they're for his eyes only. As for appearing in my PG TikTok videos, the reason he doesn't is he's just not a clout chaser, but he doesn't mind if people catch the odd sighting here and there.

The little glimpses are cool because they feed into people's feverish imagination. I literally don't have any social media accounts myself, but I'll happily participate if it means you're pursuing every opportunity and if it's best for the family.

Neither of us has ever brought anyone else home and we never will. Jackson's not really the type to sleep around, but if he *was* I'd say, good job, getting out there and socialising. My few years as a sex worker have definitely affected the way I see men. It would be hard for me to go on dates and trust a guy when I can read him like a book on first sighting. Many porn stars and OnlyFans creators have successful long-term relationships with each other, and I did once have a huge crush on a collab, with the added bonus that he completely understands our industry, but he lives in the States so it was impractical to pursue it. With our living arrangement it would be tricky if Jackson or I started seeing someone seriously, though, so at that point it would get too complicated and we'd probably have to switch to a traditional separation.

For now, we're a tight unit. Our families act as though we're still together, so invites to birthdays, Christmases and weddings are always to the two of us.

Hey, Jackson, what should I call you in this book?

Just use my name! It's in the podcast credits anyway, I can't believe nobody's noticed that.

Okay, cool. Jackson Jade it is. We're still married, after all.

~

I never want to wind up dead-eyed and uninspired, like Andrew or so many other clients. That means holding on tight to what matters. So, three years into sex work, I assigned a hefty chunk of change to the holiday of our dreams. I didn't even tell Jackson where we were going – just that we were going for a month. We both deserved it, given how hard we'd been working.

For four weeks, we ate our way through Europe: Sunday roasts in the cute Cotswolds; one of every cake at the Prada cafe in London; lemon custard sorbet and 'the most famous sandwich in the world' in Rome; ten-course degustations at Michelin-starred restaurants, where my side of the table would have to be cleared by a waiter bearing a silver crumb scraper. When we weren't stuffing our faces we lived like we were in a rom-com: vintage shopping in Notting Hill, romping around the hills of Tuscany, staying in a haunted castle in Edinburgh and swimming in the shallows of the Greek island of Milos. I got recognised a few times in London, but the most memorable occasion was at the Vatican. Yes, your humble sex worker breached the walls to visit St Peter's Basilica. It was in the queue for the Holy Door that I noticed a woman kept staring at me. Finally she came up and asked if it was really me, at which point other random women in the line gathered around, too. In these situations I quickly ask how their trip is going, before they get a chance to loudly enquire after Peggy Sue's health.

I had decided not to accept any bookings while I was away, but I did make a few custom videos, including a 4am flashing scene at the Trevi Fountain. I don't know what it is about men and ancient landmarks that make them want to ruin them. Oh, and one of my long-term clients did pay for one night in the most incredible suite at Le Meurice in Paris, overlooking the Eiffel Tower, even knowing that I was going to be rolling around in the sheets with my husband.

Jackson and I got plenty of alone time, thanks to his mum, who came with us and babysat. Cue many TikTok videos of rumpled sheets in four-poster beds and romantic tables set for two in Europe's fanciest chateaus, which drove the true-crime sleuths in the comments to absolute distraction. The biggest TikTok search for me that trip was 'Kayla Jade daddy reveal'. I suppose I can't really blame folk when I once accidentally filmed a whole podcast episode in my bedroom with a used condom in the background. Look, we're only human. Jackson is my bouncer, my best pal, my family and my sometime lover ... but I'm my own prince charming. I've created my *own* fairytale.

In a weird full-circle moment, I even wound up in the same town that the A-Lister had flown me to, what felt like a lifetime ago, though only two years had passed. On my last visit, at that freak-off by the pool, I felt like an adult, but I look back and see what a babe in the woods I was, surrounded by vacant high-profile people who had lost all lust for life. And then me, just trying to look sophisticated in my Shein dress. That was wild. *I* was wild. This time I got to check out a beautiful fifteenth-century hotel I'd heard about last trip, but on my own terms. Experiencing it with the family was a million times more fun.

Even though my job has stressed me out to the point of losing my hair, it's given me opportunities that I would never have experienced if I was still toiling away in a call centre, losing the battle of keeping my GC tan under their strip lights. People always want to know my exit plan. *Okay, so you wanted to get the bag. Haven't you got* enough *bags yet?* I'm sure one day I'll want to grow out my bush and hang up my strap-on, and I doubt I'll want to be dealing with clients' drama when I'm in the throes of perimenopause. I've heard from former sex workers that you never know when the decision to stop will come, but when it *does* come: that's it. You're done.

Right now, I'm home, sitting on my balcony in the hills of a cute country town. I won't say where it is, only that it's divinely quaint and you can *definitely* pick up some windchimes, artisan soap and fudge, or get a psychic reading. My kids will bowl through the front door in half an hour, competing to tell me about their day, but for now there's just the cluck of chickens and a distant lawn mower. Note to self: I should get a ride-on mower.

On days like this, I take a moment, log off and literally touch the grass. And I think to myself, *Damn, Kayla. Look where we are.*

Acknowledgements

Writing a book is never a solo endeavour.

To Lem Zakharia, my manager, thank you for having my back through all of this, and for helping me navigate waters I'd never swum in before.

To my publisher Kelly Doust, your unwavering support and belief in this project from day one made everything possible – thank you.

Jenny Valentish, you pushed me to dig deep, and the book is immeasurably better for it! You're a star.

Liz Robinson-Griffith kept this whole operation on track. Thank you for being the calm, organised project editor we so needed.

Brooke Lyons and Emma Schwarcz caught my errors while preserving my voice – no mean feat! Alistair Trapnell and Jasmine Aird worked their magic getting this book into the world and into the right hands, and I greatly appreciate your enthusiasm and care. To the sales team and booksellers, you're the real heroes of publishing.

To my partner and family, your love and support mean everything to me, now and always. Thank you for letting me tell my story my way. I love you.

And to readers, thank you for being willing to listen and coming along for the ride. It's been a wild one.